Managing Project Ending

"This book looks at the successful management of the premature end of one project. It uses an excellent case study and as the layers are peeled away the complexity is unveiled and the achievement of success for all parties is demonstrated. Although not couched in project management speak this is an admirable adjunct to the conventional project and programme management texts and is a recommended read for aspiring and practicing project managers."

Margaret Greenwood, University of the West of England, UK

Understanding project endings is a significant part of project management, yet there is relatively little work published in this important area. This book addresses the gap, focusing on the successful management of project endings, showing how to plan for the ending of a project, how to create ending competences, and in particular, how to successfully manage relations with different stakeholders of a project as it is coming to an end.

Havila and Salmi use a real-life case in the airline industry to show how the successful ending project was achieved and in doing so portray ideas and experiences not typically considered in the field. Through the case discussion, the complexity of the process is unveiled and the achievement of success for all parties is explained. The book portrays three key success factors: ending competences, to be developed both at the organizational and individual levels; efficient management of the business network around the ending project; and involvement at the strategic managerial level. It concludes that project endings are often complex and have far-reaching effects, and therefore, call for close managerial attention.

The book is a useful and valuable contribution both in terms of theoretical and professional practice and can be used for teaching at postgraduate, MBA and professional development levels for students engaged with project management and business strategy. In particular, this is a recommended read for top managers and for aspiring and practising project managers.

Virpi Havila is Professor of Business Studies at Uppsala University.
Asta Salmi is Professor of International Business at Helsinki School of Economics.

Routledge Advances in Management and Business Studies

Managing Project Ending

Virpi Havila and Asta Salmi

Routledge
Taylor & Francis Group

LONDON AND NEW YORK

Published 2009 by Routledge
2 Park Square, Milton Park, Abingdon, Oxon OX14 4RN
52 Vanderbilt Avenue, New York, NY 10017

First issued in paperback 2018

Routledge is an imprint of the Taylor & Francis Group, an informa business

Copyright © 2009 Virpi Havila and Asta Salmi

Notice:
Product or corporate names may be trademarks or registered trademarks, and are used only for identification and explanation without intent to infringe.

British Library Cataloguing in Publication Data
A catalogue record for this book is available from the British Library

Library of Congress Cataloging-in-Publication Data
    Havila, Virpi.
    Managing project ending / Virpi Havila and Asta Salmi.
        p. cm.
    Includes bibliographical references and index.
    ISBN 978-0-415-42337-3 (hb) — ISBN 978-0-203-88666-3 (eb)
    1. Project management. 2. Project management—Case studies. I. Salmi, Asta. II. Title.
        HD69.P75H379 2008
        658.4'04—dc22   2008023492

Typeset in Times New Roman by Pindar NZ Ltd, Auckland

ISBN 13: 978-1-138-98033-4 (pbk)
ISBN 13: 978-0-415-42337-3 (hbk)

Contents

Foreword

Managing Project Ending is a book that succeeds well in its ambition to describe the important issues that are present in key strategic decisions regarding Ending Projects, both in theory and in practice. I especially like how the authors structure the discussion around the problems and managerial issues, and provide examples of these through extracts from this real-life empirical case. Having been involved as one of the decision-makers in the empirical case – that of terminating long-term interorganisational co-operation on production of civil aircraft – I was delighted to see how well the authors succeed in describing and analysing the actual processes involved in this complex Ending Project. The book is instructive, easy to read and exciting. Termination of projects is a challenge that many managers encounter. This book gives both project managers and general managers valuable advice on how to overcome the challenges.

Gert Schyborger, CEO, SAAB Aircraft AB, 1997–99

Acknowledgements

We would like to express our warmest thanks to all the managers interviewed for this book. Many people from several companies made time in their busy schedules to discuss endings from their own perspective. Without these managers' willingness to share their knowledge and experiences with us, this book would not exist. We are also grateful to the interviewees for reading and commenting on different versions of the manuscript. The many helpful suggestions we received are highly appreciated.

In addition to the managers involved, other people have taken their time to review drafts of the manuscript. Our sincere thanks are due to Dr Peter Dahlin, Managing Director Tuija Lindblad and Professor Rolf Lundin, whose detailed and well-informed comments helped us to clarify our points. We also extend our gratitude to Professor Helén Anderson, who gave us the initial idea for this project and the contacts needed for its implementation; to Dr Catherine Welch, who has supported the project in many ways; to Project Manager Seppo Salmi, MSc., who shared his professional experiences of terminating projects; and to Sheryl Hinkkanen, MA, who, by improving the fluency of our English, helped us in ending the book project. All of you have helped us to present important managerial insights eloquently in this book. The remaining errors are ours.

Financial support from the Swedish–Finnish Cultural Foundation and Tore Browaldhs Stiftelse is gratefully acknowledged. We also extend our gratitude to Saab AB for granting the permission to reproduce the photographs in this book.

Virpi Havila and Asta Salmi

Introduction

Our approach to projects

Attention to project endings

There is certainly no lack of books dealing with project management. One can easily find practical guides and handbooks offering advice on how to manage projects efficiently as well as scientific studies analysing the intrinsic features of projects; there are even books devoted to special types of projects. The reason for the great interest is, of course, that we all live in a world of projects.

Most project management texts are structured around the project life-cycle. This seems natural, as projects by definition have specific goals intended to be reached within a given time, so both readers and instructors are most comfortable with this arrangement.[1] In addition, the life-cycle concept seems to provide a comprehensive and balanced approach to all the critical stages of a project, from its initiation to its end. In practice, however, most attention has been paid to the starting and planning phases, while project closure has been discussed rather too little.

Only a small fraction of the discussion in the literature is devoted to the ending of a project. In a typical textbook, for instance, fewer than 5 per cent of pages discuss the phase of ending a project. Still more importantly, the writings thus far assume that ending a project is self-evident and without problems. Indeed, given the vast literature on project management, we have been surprised to see how little attention has been given to *project termination*. Our own research results and the empirical case in this book have led us to believe that there is a need for much more reflection on project endings.

Projects are popular because they are appealing to managers. Once set, project deadlines focus attention and mobilise action. Starting a project is also a way to show, both internally and externally, that something is in the process of improving. Furthermore, projects are seemingly easy to handle and execute, as long as they are well planned and properly resourced beforehand. However, we know from experience that many projects last longer and cost more than had been planned, or they encounter problems owing to the fact that the resulting quality does not meet the set criteria. In our view, the basic definition of projects as something with a simple end has been taken at face value. Since there has been almost no problematisation of the ending phase, texts fail to give *managerial guidance* for this critical aspect of project management.

Project management with a contextual view

The project management literature has given increasing attention to the wider contexts in which projects take place. In 1995, Kreiner[2] pointed out the importance of consideration for the environment of a project during project planning and execution. Given the rapidly changing global business environment, the need for a contextual view of projects is becoming increasingly important. We propose the adoption of a contextual view and, more specifically, we concentrate on the *network context of projects*.

We propose that project ending may have wider effects on the environment of a project than has been realised so far. This, in turn, has important implications for successful project termination and thus calls for managerial attention. For instance, managers need to understand, as expressed by Håkansson and Snehota[3] that 'no business is an island', in the sense that what happens in a company's relation with one customer may influence what happens in its relations with other customers or suppliers. It therefore becomes important to understand the *connectedness of the relations of a company*.[4] Our empirical case will clearly show the importance of understanding the connectedness between the different stakeholders involved in a project.

Increasingly, managers need not only monitor developments around their company; they also need to develop skills for managing relations with different stakeholders. Here, we focus on the skills and capabilities related to the termination of a project; in particular; we focus on *project-ending competences*. Furthermore, to advance managerial thinking, we formulate the complex ending process as a project of its own. We propose that when a project ending is tricky or complicated, the wise manager constructs the situation into a new project: *an Ending Project*. As will be shown, the processes of ending mean that the ending of a project has special features (such as timing problems and changes in atmosphere, organisation and commitment) that make its management challenging.

A case study on management of the ending

This book focuses on the critical processes that are present in the termination of complex projects. We base our discussion on a real-life case. We present an empirical case in the airline industry, where a large-scale interorganisational Ending Project was implemented. We show how complex project endings cannot be left only to the project management. Since various project stakeholders may play a key role in the processes of ending, both the strategies and operations related to the termination must involve the general management. This book is a story of two excellent products: the Saab 340 and 2000 aircrafts. All parties involved in the development and production of these products expected them both to be sales successes. The Saab 340 lived up to these expectations and met with success, whereas production of the Saab 2000 was halted after five years, when only sixty-three planes had been produced. Our discussion shows that the ending of these product lines was an unexpected and complicated process. We also illustrate that despite the failure of the product, the company, Saab Aircraft AB, managed the Ending Project successfully. The aircraft industry has its own special features, owing to the fact that the planning horizons are long; aircrafts are investments that need spare parts and maintenance as long as they are in use, which is usually around twenty-five to thirty years. This means that the manufacturer and the suppliers of components continue to be tied to the products even though new products are no longer produced. To understand this case and its environment, we discuss the connected business relationships and actors, i.e. the business network in which the case company is embedded.[5]

The empirical case represents an efficient Ending Project involving several actors and stakeholders. It is an interesting case as it illustrates a 'success story' – thus providing good examples for managerial actions, or even best practices for adoption by other managers. Furthermore, the case is important, as it is real: developments are discussed openly, thanks to the company representatives who were willing to disclose them.[6]

The book is structured around the developments of the empirical case: the Ending Project. Each chapter focuses on a certain aspect of project termination and the related management issues, thus considering in turn each facet of the many-sided case and illustrating the complexities involved. The case shows how managers acted in practice and how their strategies concerning the relations with the different stakeholders evolved. We conclude each chapter with a summary of the key managerial takeaways.

Who is this book for?

This book addresses a wide managerial audience: from project managers to general managers, and from strategic planners to individuals who need to develop their project-ending competences. While the conventional project management theories that focus on project life-cycles, sophisticated project management tools and planning retain their central position, our perspective, with its focus on the environmental effects of project termination, provides valuable new ideas on how to handle the ending phases of projects efficiently. The book thus makes valuable reading for aspiring project managers.

The key starting point of our book is that project managers should not bear the sole responsibility for terminating complex projects when they end in a premature or unplanned manner. When a project starts to run over time and over budget, and especially when it has many external stakeholders, the strategic decision-makers – often even the CEOs – should be involved in the process. The handbooks and practical guides now available usually lack this view: the strategic level and top management are typically mentioned only with regard to the starting and planning phases. The role of general management is limited to helping project managers define the initial project goals, and does not include helping them to overcome the problems posed by a premature project ending. However, the latter may call for much more strategy formulation and many actions in order to ensure future business. Indeed, the lack of attention to project termination may well be the reason why problems are faced in future projects. It is enjoyable and motivating to start new projects, but it is a real challenge to terminate a project in a successful way and thus to ensure that the initial, and often considerable, investments will pay off. The people carrying out the demanding and difficult job of ending projects need much support and deserve credit from their superiors so that they are strong enough to endure the processes involved.

We expect this book to be valuable for researchers in the fields of business studies, crisis management and project management. For instance, our discussion on temporality and contextuality may be taken further, and our deep and extensive case description gives room for investigations from other perspectives. We concentrate on supplier relations, but the case also reports on network dynamics more generally. The book is also valuable reading for use in managerial education and training.

Notes

1 Mantel, S. J. *et al.* (2001) *Project Management in Practice*, New York: John Wiley & Sons, p. viii.
2 Kreiner, K. (1995) 'In Search of Relevance: Project Management in Drifting Environments', *Scandinavian Journal of Management*, 11, 335–46.
3 Håkansson, H. and Snehota, I. (1989) 'No Business Is an Island: The Network Concept of Business Strategy', *Scandinavian Journal of Management*, 22, 256–70.
4 Connections have been discussed by, for instance, Anderson, J. C., Håkansson, H. and Johanson, J. (1994) 'Dyadic Business Relationships within a Business

Network Context', *Journal of Marketing*, 58, 1–15; Halinen, A., Salmi, A. and Havila, V. (1999) 'From Dyadic Change to Changing Business Networks: An Analytical Framework', *Journal of Management Studies*, 36, 779–94.

5   For further discussion on business networks, see, e.g., Ford, D. (1998) *Managing Business Relationships*, Chichester, UK: Wiley, and the website of the Industrial Marketing and Purchasing Group, http://www.impgroup.org.

6   For the case study, thirteen persons at different levels and in different involved companies in four countries were interviewed. These included Saab Aircraft AB, some of its key suppliers and one of its customers. The interviews were conducted between April 1999 and March 2000. The book manuscript was read and commented on in 2008 by three managers of the SAAB Group. In addition, we have made extensive use of written material, including documents and publications, concerning the companies and their products.

1 Ending a project

More than project closure

In this chapter, we briefly describe the intrinsic features of projects and strive to show how and why their termination may be difficult. We start by focusing on the complexities that may be present (Introduction). We then briefly discuss key features of projects and their life cycles (What is a project?), thus showing how project termination is typically handled in the project management literature. Next, we present the specific difficulties encountered in project termination (Project termination is difficult), before describing our key suggestions as to how these difficulties are best tackled (How should a project be terminated?). We introduce our case study (The Ending Project) then conclude with the important key points for managers.

Introduction

Managing through projects has become common in business, and many managers are involved in numerous small and large projects simultaneously. These projects may vary markedly in their importance and length, or by their nature and aims. To name only a few, there are new product launches, IT application projects with both developmental and maintenance phases, training projects, construction projects and organisation restructuring projects. These projects have deadlines that give rhythm to the manager's life – once a project is closed, a new one starts or has already started.

Projects are usually related to something planned, well defined and controlled. This also makes them attractive for managers: projects seem 'to be easier to control, delimit, terminate and follow up. [...] Thus, the proliferation of projects harmonizes well with a striving for action, visibility, and evaluation', as Sahlin-Andersson and Söderholm have noted.[1] Organising tasks into a project gives the feeling that the tasks are being completed efficiently.

But the closure of a project is not always as easy as expected, nor does it always take place when expected. This book is about managing such situations. To illustrate the complexities of ending, we present a real-life case describing the premature termination of a production programme. This termination was done by reconfiguring the situation into that of a new type of project: an Ending Project. Along with presentation of the Ending Project, we focus on various central aspects of termination.

It is difficult to bring unsuccessful projects to a close,[2] but according to Staw and Ross,[3] '... good management consists of knowing when to pull the plug'. Their advice concerns both actions that executives can take themselves (for instance, recognising over-commitment) and actions that call for changes in the organisation (such as replacing project managers or improving information systems). One also finds advice in the literature on practical implementation of the closing phase of a project, for example, what kind of documents should be filled in and filed.[4] However, so far the project management literature lacks deeper *strategic thinking* on how to end a project successfully.

To start with, we examine what typical projects look like, and then summarise the key points of our approach to projects.

What is a project?

There is certainly no lack of literature on project management. Several books discuss projects in general, while others focus on specific types of projects, such as product development projects, project marketing, or construction projects. In addition, one can easily find practical guidebooks. All these texts start out from a more or less similar definition of a project.

Definition of a project

In general usage, a project implies that something gets done. More specifically, a project is often defined by the task it is supposed to complete during a specified time and with specific resources. For example, the Project Management Institute (PMI) defines projects as '... a temporary endeavor undertaken to create a unique product or service, or result'.[5]

To define what projects are in more detail, let us examine the key features usually listed for projects. The project management literature is full of more or less similar examples of these listings, a typical one being the following description by Field and Keller:[6]

A project
*   is a unique undertaking
*   has specific objectives/goals to achieve
*   requires resources

- has a budget
- has a schedule
- involves human resources and efforts of people, and
- its success can be measured in terms of how closely it comes to meeting its goal; thus measures of quality apply.

All projects are by definition limited in time; they should be brought to a close on a specific date or during a specific period that is set in advance. This means that as soon as the task, project budget and project team are known, the deadline and the end of the project are known as well. Time pressures are usually tough and the deadline comes too soon; as noted by Lundin and Söderholm, 'time is always running out since it is finite from the start, limited for instance by contracts or other conditions.'[7] Therefore, temporality is a key defining factor for projects – they are not meant to be permanent.

What constitutes a project is, however, very much a practical issue, too. This became evident in our discussions with the managers of the empirical case. The persons interviewed used the word 'project' in many different ways and often differently from the standard textbook definitions. Activities around both the Saab 340 and the Saab 2000 initially constituted product development projects and prototype production projects. The interesting question is whether they were 'projects' during the period of our analysis, that is, when the production lines were being closed down. Several of the persons interviewed discuss the situation as if projects, not on-going (permanent) manufacturing operations, were being closed down. This shows the present business world's tendency to formulate tasks as projects. It also shows that managers constantly need to cope with interlinked and partly simultaneous projects of different nature. It is therefore not surprising that little room is left for thinking about the challenges arising in ending some of these projects.

Project life-cycle

Projects are often defined by their timing: In the words of Lundin and Söderholm, they are 'starting with the initiation and ending with evaluation'.[8] Between its initiation and ending, a project can be seen to follow a life-cycle.[9] The basic life-cycle includes the following four phases: Initiation, Development, Implementation and Termination.

All projects are different and therefore the project life-cycles may also differ.[10] For example, some projects do not have an explicit closure phase, but instead they fade out and are finally forgotten. But in general terms, the key four phases of the project life-cycle are the following.

Initiation phase

This phase starts with *project definition* and relates the work of the project to the project owner's business objectives, and thus also to strategic planning. In this book we use the expression *project owner* to indicate that it is the organisation that 'owns' the project and thus makes the 'go/no-go' decision for the project. Other terms that are often used in the same context are *project customer* and *client*.

When initiating a project, the project owner needs to define the purpose of the project as well as the expected output. Depending on the type of project, this may mean the development of a new product, launching a new product, a new organisational structure, or a new building. The project owner also needs to decide on the scope of the project so that it is clear when the project is completed. This means that it must be clear what quality should be reached, what budget limits exist and when the project should be finished. According to Lock, a 'golden rule [...] is to define and document the project in all respects before the estimates are made and translated into budgets and price'.[11]

Development phase

When the project owner has made the 'go' decision, it is time to start planning the project in more detail. The next decision is to appoint a *project manager* who will be responsible for the planning and execution. The following major tasks are important to include in the detailed planning:[12]

- identification of tasks
- sequencing of the activities in the project
- identification of activities critical to success
- choosing the type of project organisation and project team
- estimating costs
- budgeting
- time scheduling
- evaluation methods.

The process of project planning should be documented in a *project plan*. How extensive the plan should be depends on the type of project. One purpose of the project plan is to show both internally and externally who are working on the project, when they are going to deliver and what they are supposed to deliver. Another purpose is to help the project manager to follow the progress of the work.

Implementation phase

During the implementation phase, it is the project manager's task to lead the project towards the project goal. The following key activities are usually important during this phase:

- communicating with the project owner and the various stakeholders
- selecting suppliers
- reviewing progress
- monitoring costs
- controlling quality
- issuing orders for change
- managing changes
- motivating project team members.

There are numerous guidebooks where a project manager can find help about how to manage a project. For instance, there are guidelines on how to budget and estimate costs, how to schedule a project, and how to control it; the techniques explained in the literature include such as PERT, CPM, and GANTT.[13] There are also many books that focus especially on developing the skills needed by a project manager to manage the project, and even guidelines on managing problems that might come up.

Termination phase

The termination phase starts with a formal termination decision and announcement. Meredith and Mantel[14] suggest that project termination should be planned, budgeted and scheduled in the same way as the other phases that arise during the life-cycle of a project. Several textbooks recommend a project termination checklist.[15] The management is typically advised to follow standard administrative procedures in project closure.

During this phase, the *project work is finalised*, with the goal being to finish the work within the set time, at the set cost and according to the specified quality requirements. According to Turner,[16] the tasks of this phase include, for instance, frequent controls to ensure the completion of all tasks, planning for the run-down of the project team, closing contracts with suppliers and subcontractors, and closing the project's accounts so that no further charging to the project is possible. Care of the project team is especially important, as the team's performance may drop. One reason for this is that the team members may already have mentally started to plan for the future.[17]

In some projects, the termination phase also includes planning for the *transfer from project manager to operations manager.*[18] This means that the project is definitely closed and that the responsibilities and ownership are transferred to the operation manager or customer. The transfer means that it is made clear who is responsible for the possible maintenance needed in the future. The termination phase also includes a *project evaluation*. The purpose of the evaluation is to give feedback to the project owner about, for example, whether or not the project has reached the expected goals with regard to time, cost and quality, and what lessons can be learnt.[19] With a view to future projects, it is important to know the specific factors that led to success or failure.

Finally, it is important *to record* all the descriptions of the project design, technical data and possible drawings including all changes during the project.[20] Another important decision to make is how to store all the documents, which may contain information needed when planning the next project. A *final report* describing the project and the whole process, with comments on project performance, should end the termination phase.

This discussion shows that project termination is a key stage of the project life-cycle, and that project planning usually includes the plan for project termination. The project management literature notes that ending is important: in the words of Turner, the end of the project is 'the second most critical stage of a project. Nobody remembers effective start-up, but everyone remembers ineffective close-out; the consequences are to be seen for a long time.'[21]

In spite of all this, however, we see two specific lacks in the project management literature published so far. Firstly, most of the attention is directed to the early phases of projects, and little is said about their termination. Secondly, little attention is paid to the fact that the termination phase differs from the other project phases. For example, Turner[22] points out that 'the skills required to finish a project can be different to those required to start it up and run it' and further, '... it may be appropriate to change managers in the final stage'. To reveal the special features of Ending Projects, this book concentrates on the phase of project termination.

A key question then emerges: What is 'ending' and when does it take place? While some activities are terminated, they may immediately lead to others. Or the initial activities may be re-started after a while. Our case study illustrates clearly that as far as complex projects are concerned, different endings take place at different points in time. In our case, two production lines were closed down, which meant that no new commercial aircraft were produced. However, this did not mean the end of business as the company still owned 310 aircraft: it continued to lease them and also to sell spare parts and maintenance for the whole existing fleet.

Indeed, project life-cycles seem increasingly to include new phases, such as after-sales, marketing and maintenance, thus making them longer than before. In particular, concern over environmental responsibility pushes companies to consider longer product life-cycles, including, for example, recycling of materials. This probably means even longer and more complex project life-cycles as well, thus raising the need for a thorough understanding of different project phases. Our focus on the ending phase and its special features should in fact help managers even more generally to understand the versatile nature of projects in their various phases.

Project termination is difficult

The project management literature, with a few exceptions,[23] usually gives the picture that project termination is something important, natural and uncomplicated. In practice, project termination is often more difficult than was assumed when the project started.

Firstly, managers have a tendency to cling to projects that are beyond hope and should in fact be dropped. Secondly, it may be difficult to know when to terminate a project. Finally, a project is not a closed system. This means that, especially during the termination phase, it is important and often necessary to inform the various stakeholders and negotiate with them. This, in turn, makes the termination even more complicated.

In this section, we briefly introduce the reader to the key issues that may cause problems when starting the termination phase. The issues we highlight all show that managers should in fact be much more active in deliberating whether to end projects and when, and further, that someone needs to take the initial step to begin discussion on project termination more often than is now being done. In many cases, such talks are not launched by the project manager. We shall approach these issues, suggesting the steps the project manager and the project owner might take to ensure a successful project termination.

Failure or success?

It is not easy to decide to terminate a project that has failed to reach the goals set for it in advance. The reasons for this are psychological (managers tend to see only what is in line with their beliefs), social (it is difficult to expose mistakes to others) and structural (administrative and organisational inertia is at play here).[24]

It is also difficult to know whether a project that appears to be a failure at a given moment in time will continue to be perceived as a failure in the future. Engwall[25] uses the Opera House in Sydney as an example of a project that seemed to be a failure but later proved to be a success. The project was a disaster as it went over budget and exceeded its time limits, and the building turned out to be much smaller than had originally been planned. However, today it is as famous and important to Sydney as the Eiffel Tower is to Paris. Furthermore, a project is not isolated from its context, nor is it a closed system. Many individuals and organisations may have a stake in the project. Some of these, such as the project owner and the project team, are obvious. Moreover, the most direct external stakeholders, such as customers and/ or suppliers, are easily recognised. In addition, there are less obvious but equally important parties to consider. We shall return to this contextual issue in the coming chapters.

Timing of termination

The project management literature pays little attention to when the termination phase starts or should start. Since projects are seen to follow life-cycles that end with project termination, there is 'a built-in termination mechanism'.[26] The question is how well this built-in mechanism actually works in real life.

A project manager can face four different situations when terminating a project:

- termination according to plan
- premature termination
- late termination
- non-termination.

Termination according to plan is the easiest situation to handle, as in such situations the project has succeeded in reaching its goals with regard to budget, time and quality, and can therefore be terminated as planned. However, we know from practice that in spite of good preparations, aims and motivations, many projects fail to reach the quality set during the initiation phase. Many projects also exceed their budgets. Some of these projects are terminated earlier than planned, others later than planned.

The advice given in literature is that the project management should end the project if it does not reach the goals set in advance. For example, Davis argues that senior executives should abandon a project if the costs go heavily over budget. Before abandoning a project, senior executives are advised to have an independent management team study whether re-costing would be possible: 'When an overrun becomes serious, the only sensible recourse is to rework the project from the ground up and, if necessary, either abandon or rebudget'.[27]

Lock[28] gives some examples that may call for *premature termination*:

- the project has been completed earlier than planned

- the project owner has run out of funds
- the project owner changes the project's purpose and expected output
- the project owner's situation changes owing to economic or political changes.

The project management literature thus recognises that premature termination sometimes must take place. There is, however, no guide on how to deal with premature termination, no advice, for example, as to what sort of activities would be critical for the project manager to consider.

The project management literature has dealt with *late termination*, owing to the view of projects as a time-linked phenomenon. If a project is not finished in time, according to Lundin and Söderholm it is: '... regarded as just as disastrous as a bankruptcy would be in an ordinary firm'.[29] Again, what is missing in the literature is how the project manager should deal with late termination.

The fourth situation, *non-termination*, is a situation that the project management literature maintains cannot occur, as termination is included in the planning of the project. In reality, however, some projects fade out and in the end are simply forgotten. Other non-terminated projects are transformed into a new project/projects without the first project having been brought to a clear end.

How should a project be terminated?

This book will show that termination of a project in itself becomes a project: it is *an Ending Project*. Such a project has a time limit, a purpose and specific resources; furthermore, the ending process should involve both external parties and the upper echelons of the company. Terminating a project is often a strategic decision that calls for careful consideration.

The key managerial topic to be addressed in this book then is: How is termination managed? Briefly, the chapters that follow will focus on the network context of projects, the need to plan termination, the creation of ending competence, management of the project's environment, and the success factors for project termination. These are introduced next.

Projects take place in business networks

Many individuals and organisations have a stake in the success of a project. Firstly, all the individuals working within the project and secondly, all the individuals and organisations in the project's environment. In situations when the project lasts longer, costs more and/or the quality does not meet the set criteria, it becomes especially important to identify the stakeholders.[30] Examples of project stakeholders are customers, suppliers, project sponsors, managers and local citizens.

In our view, the project and its ending may also affect other parties – those connected with the key stakeholders. Thus we shall look at the network context of the project. Since the network context of each project is unique, its management can only be based on the involved managers' own analysis of the stakeholders and involvement in the relations.

If the project is an interorganisational co-operation project, the ending decision simultaneously influences many organisations both directly and indirectly. This means, too, that co-operation is needed when terminating a project. Thus, managing the ending is more than a job for planners and schedulers; it should involve also the general management of the involved company/companies.

Planning the ending strategy

The ending strategy involves the planning and execution of the plans from the point when the company first realises the potential need to end the project to the point when the project has been terminated and the ending has been evaluated. It therefore has three key elements: realisation of the need to end a project; planning of the Ending Project; and execution of the Ending Project. This also means that the decision-makers at the strategic level need to be involved in the process.

Especially when a project does not meet its goals with regard to timing, costs and/or quality, the project management should focus on project ending and should plan for a specific Ending Project. Termination is a project in itself that calls for planning in the same way as the initial project, including time limits and resources.

According to Spirer and Hamburger,[31] project termination may cause both emotional and intellectual problems. These may concern the project staff as well as the project client. Furthermore, the problems may be internal, relating to the internal processes of the project, or external, relating to, for instance, stakeholders. Spirer and Hamburger note that since loss of interest is likely to characterise the termination phase, this should be treated as a project:

> Make it clear that closeout has its own project identity. Some project managers give the closeout its own project name. 'Start-up' meetings for the beginning of termination help establish the concept that there is a well-defined goal to be met – closing out the job properly.
>
> (1988, p. 239)

It is surprising how rarely this piece of advice seems to be followed!

Project-ending competences

A successful Ending Project means, for instance, that negative feelings are kept to a minimum and the parties can continue to co-operate in other ways. The ending of one project does not necessarily mean that the parties cease to co-operate with one another. They may continue with a new project, or they may have a business relationship. Our discussion will show how critical it was in the real-life case to give various stakeholders accurate information in a timely manner. Indeed, it illustrates how this open communication led to fruitful business interaction rather than frustrated business partners and ill-will. In essence, there are important lessons to be learnt regarding the competences required.

By *project-ending competences* we mean abilities and skills of both the organisation and its employees to run down the project so that the stakeholders involved incur as little harm as possible. This creates success in project termination, despite the fact that the termination itself takes place in an originally unplanned or premature manner.

A solid basis for this competence is formed by the visions of the managers at the strategic level, above individual project managers or project teams. Implementation of the ending, in turn, involves managers and people at lower organisational levels, as well as project stakeholders. Thus, several of the individuals involved need project-ending competences. We shall also discuss how the company can create and enhance project-ending competences.

The ending means managing changes in different relations

Our discussion will show how different partners need to be approached differently, at the same time acknowledging their interconnections. For instance, in our case study, the suppliers were also sharing information amongst themselves, so it was critical that all the information they received from the key company was consistent and accurate.

Moreover, we note that different stakeholders may see the network and relations differently, and in consequence they form different pictures of the network. These pictures affect how they react to the Ending Project. It is therefore central that the Ending Project manager maintains the key resources of the project until its end; also important are to manage a new type of a team – the project-ending organisation – and to manage all the various relations with stakeholders at the same time.

Success in ending

This book will show that, aside from efficient individuals, the success factors for an Ending Project are team work, communication, management of relationships and a holistic view of the surrounding environment, i.e. the business network. So that all these factors contribute to a positive outcome, companies should pay more attention to forming good strategies for ending and to accumulating ending competences.

Essentially, a successful ending calls for company-specific, project-specific and relationship-specific ending knowledge. We therefore note that, while helpful, it is not enough to hire an 'exit champion'[32] or a 'termination manager'[33]. Furthermore, successful ending requires attention from both Ending Project management and the general management. While the former needs to tackle all the practicalities of the stressful situation, the latter is needed essentially to take decisions and provide fundamental support for the process.

The Ending Project: a case study from the aircraft industry

Throughout this book we will follow a two-and-a-half-year-long Ending Project, namely how the Swedish company, Saab Aircraft AB, managed termination of the production of its commercial aircraft. The story starts a year before the final decision to terminate was taken and ends when all of the contracts with the more than 200 suppliers had been either terminated or renegotiated.

In all, some 300 companies were directly affected by the termination of production, which meant that the ending process was somewhat complicated. The situation was further complicated by the fact that the decision also meant the premature ending of a production programme.

An aircraft is a product that has a long life, around twenty-five to thirty years, and throughout its lifetime, each individual airplane must be in perfect shape, equipped with modern technical equipment. Therefore, even though the production of new aircraft ended, the need to produce spare parts and to provide maintenance did not. This, in turn, means that the Ending Project was very important for Saab Aircraft AB. As will be seen, the managers of this company were very skilful in their management of the Ending Project, which also explains why this particular real-life case is used in this book. We need good examples of how termination is managed successfully. So, ladies and gentlemen, it's time for take-off and to a more detailed look at our aircraft!

To make it easy to follow developments concerning the case, we have organised our empirical discussion into separate boxes. In Box 1.1: Starting the termination phase, we shall describe the tricky situation facing company decision-makers at the beginning of 1997.

Box 1.1 is also an illustration of the problems that arise as far as the timing of termination is concerned. At that time, the company produced two commercial aircraft types: the Saab 340 and the Saab 2000. The Saab 340 was an old product that had been a sales success. The production of the second aircraft type, the Saab 2000, came to an end in 1999, after a mere five years of development and production, when only sixty-three airplanes had been produced. All the parties directly involved – the suppliers, the launching customer and the manufacturer's employees – had expected the aircraft to become a sales success similar to that of the Saab 340. But that did not happen.

Box 1.1 Starting the termination phase

Saab AB: a producer with long experience

Saab AB is a Swedish company established in 1937. Since the company was founded, it has designed fifteen different aircraft types and produced more than 4,000 aircraft. This means that the company has long experience within the aircraft industry. Saab AB is also seen to be among the leaders with regard to safe commercial aircraft. As expressed by one of its managers: 'Saab has been successful and is better in keeping its aircraft in the air than several of its competitors with a similar aircraft type.'

The history of Swedish aircraft production goes back to 1936, when the Swedish Government decided to work to establish a domestic defence industry. A new company, Svenska Aeroplan AB (later called Saab), was set up in 1937 and started to build military aircraft. When the Second World War was about to end in 1944, Saab started the development of commercial aircraft. Its first commercial aircraft, the Saab 90 Scandia, accommodated between twenty-four and thirty-two passengers. Production of the Saab 90 Scandia was cancelled after only eighteen aircraft had been produced. The reason for the cancellation of production was due the Swedish Government's decision to focus entirely on military production.

It took about thirty years until Saab AB again became active on the commercial aircraft market, when Saab AB and Fairchild Industries of the USA started to co-operate on developing a twin-turboprop regional airliner for about thirty passengers. At the time there were only airplanes with eighty seats, and the two companies had noticed that there was a need for a smaller aircraft.

The first prototype of the plane, called the Saab–Fairchild SF-340, made its maiden flight on 25 January 1983, three years after co-

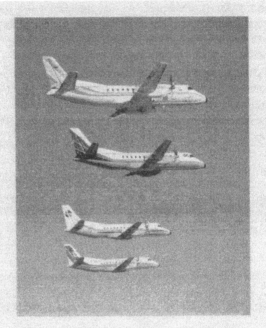

Figure 1.1 The Saab 340. Photo courtesy of Saab AB.

operation between Saab and Fairchild was launched. In 1984 Fairchild decided to withdraw from the project and Saab took over; from then on, the aircraft was called the Saab 340.

In 1999, when production ceased, Saab AB had a third of the world market segment for smaller aircraft. The business unit within Saab AB that handled the production of commercial aircraft in the 1990s was called Saab Aircraft AB. In all, 459 Saab 340 aircraft had been produced between 1984 and 1999. (See Figure 1.1: The Saab 340.)

All involved parties recouped their development costs, which in turn means that no one questioned Saab Aircraft's decision to cease producing the Saab 340; it was seen as a 'natural death'. As one manager at Saab Aircraft AB put it: 'All manufacturing programmes of this kind are terminated sooner or later [...]. One runs this or that many hundred, and no one questions it or calls it "cessation". Instead it merely "expires", as it is called.'

At the time of the decision to start development of a new product, all the parties involved agreed that the right decision was taken. One of the managers involved pointed out that when 'the decision was taken [...] as to how the Saab 2000 aircraft should look, all the actors on the market agreed that a turboprop aircraft was the right type to develop. Everyone! No one returned to the matter later and said that [...] you made the wrong decision in 1989.'

An excellent product but ...

Saab Aircraft AB had its successful product, the Saab 340, in mind when the company decided to develop an aircraft that could carry up to fifty passengers. The idea underlying the larger aircraft was that operators flying the Saab 340 would get a new product to grow into.

The first plans for the new aircraft, the Saab 2000, were presented on 15 December 1988. This new aircraft was planned to be the fastest turboprop airplane on the market, with a speed of 670 km/h and range of 2,340 km. It was also planned to be more passenger-friendly, with a more spacious interior and 'generous seat and aisle widths, plus excellent headroom'. Passenger comfort would also be enhanced by slow-turning propellers that would guarantee a low noise level in the cabin. At that stage, nothing seemed to indicate anything but another successful product. The new aircraft would be as the Saab 340, but bigger and better in several aspects.

The new aircraft, the Saab 2000, was seen as superior to competing products. For example, the Swedish producer, Saab Aircraft AB, presented a long list of all the requirements that its product, the commercial aircraft Saab 2000, met and why it was superior to other turboprops and jets in the regional aircraft market:

• higher speed and longer range
• better economics than regional jets or conventional turboprops
• lower block times and higher flight levels
• higher rates of climb
• outstanding manoeuvrability and excellent airfield performance
• lower interior and exterior noise levels
• active noise control

For the customers, i.e. regional operators worldwide, the new product would mean better economy, as the Saab 2000 would be able to offer better range and speed. Or, as the Saab Aircraft AB website (Saab Aircraft. Product information: Saab 2000 1999-03-25) put it: 'The Saab 2000 has the range and speed to offer regional airlines greater productivity with superb economics. Jet-like performance with up to 370 knots cruise speed, a service ceiling of 31,000 ft and rapid rates of climb combine to provide a high degree of operational flexibility.'

The first customer and launching partner, the regional airliner Crossair, agreed with Saab Aircraft AB that the product was superior because of the economy of the aircraft's operation: 'The concept of the Saab 2000 is very good. It is brilliant […] It is fast, it climbs high, it is comfortable.' Crossair was the first customer to purchase the Saab 2000, and eventually it also became the last one to receive the aircraft. (See Figure 1.2 for the Saab 2000.) Crossair served as a regional hub, and therefore needed smaller aircraft. The prototype of the Saab 2000 was ready at the end of 1991. (See Figure 1.2, The first flight, 26 March 1992.)

Crossair started to operate the Saab 2000 in August 1994, and the last Saab 2000 was delivered to Crossair on 29 April 1999.

Figure 1.2 The first flight, 26 March 1992. Photo courtesy of Saab AB.

… there was a premature and complex end to production

When production stopped, Saab Aircraft AB had only produced sixty-three Saab 2000 aircraft. The Saab 2000 never became the same success story its 'little sister', the Saab 340, had been. The premature termination meant that the parties involved would now be forced to share the risk they took when co-operation began.

It was very difficult to decide to stop the production of the Saab 2000 after only sixty-three airplanes had been made. To recoup all the investment costs that Saab Aircraft AB, its suppliers and its launching customer had put into the development of the new model would have required the production of at least 200 aircraft. Moreover, it is more expensive to manufacture the first units, because more working hours are needed per unit. As only sixty-three Saab 2000 were manufactured, the suppliers' manufacturing costs never reached the normal level on which the price of the components had been based. In most cases, this normal level is reached after 100 units or so.

For all the suppliers involved in development of the Saab 2000, the cessation of production was a disappointment. It was not what the parties involved had expected would happen. As one of Saab Aircraft AB's managers stated: 'Everyone [...] had expected to be able to produce at least a few hundred of the aircraft'.

But why did Saab Aircraft AB only produce sixty-three aircraft?

Potential customers wanted to 'wait and see'

Some technical problems occurred during development of the Saab 2000, which delayed launching of the aircraft. One problem, which surfaced during test flights with the first aircraft, involved the flight characteristics. It was decided to change the mechanical pitch control system (MECS, Mechanical Elevator Control System) to a system where the elevator was power controlled through an electrical input (PECS, Powered Elevator Control System). This change from a mechanical to a hydraulic control system took about a year, as a large number of parts and tools had to be redesigned. In addition, several of the suppliers were involved. For example, it took the supplier of the tail for the Saab 2000 several months to redesign components and tools.

This together with the fact that some technical problems had occurred in the early development of the Saab 340 may have influenced potential customers to 'wait and see', letting others do the costly development work. According to one person at Crossair's technical department: 'Many customers who had the Saab 340 said, "I'm going to look first before I buy the 2000 [...] I'll wait until they're here and then I'll buy. I'm not going to make all these modifications."'

The parties involved can only speculate whether or not the product would have been a sales success had the launching not been delayed. One of the managers at a Finnish supplier company remembers that it 'was a topic of speculation whether the one-year delay had an impact [...]. It probably happened at the same time when [...] jets of the same size began to arrive on the market.'

Fierce competition resulting in low prices

The aircraft industry is divided into two: manufacturers producing large aircraft from 100 seats and upwards, and those producing the so-called regional aircraft. In 1997, following structural changes, only two producers remained in the first group: Boeing and Airbus. They turned out, in total, around 700–800 aircraft per year, and had together about 95 per cent of the total commercial aircraft market.

The regional aircraft market, on which Saab Aircraft AB was competing, accounts for the remaining 5 per cent. In 1997 there were six producers competing in this segment, which was characterised by considerable overcapacity: the six companies had an annual production capacity of about 800 aircraft, but only some 200 were built each year. This meant that there was fierce competition between the companies, and the way to compete was to offer lower prices. During the 1990s, Saab Aircraft AB had sold aircraft at prices below production costs. During a four-year period, for instance, Saab Aircraft AB had made a loss of 4 billion Swedish crowns.

This left Saab AB with only one alternative: to leave this market before more money was lost. As the Managing Director of Saab Aircraft AB expressed it: 'It is very clear when you look at it from the outside.'

'Jets are modern, propellers are old-fashioned', thinks the passenger

Soon after Saab Aircraft AB started to launch its new turboprop aircraft, several competitors introduced jet aircraft of the same size as Saab's regional aircraft. Jets started to gain more market share even though turboprop aircraft was more economical to use than jets. As one manager at Saab Aircraft AB said, regional jets had 'high acquisition costs [...], were expensive to operate and maintain [...], and more often require better paid pilots'. The reason seemed to be that the passengers appreciated jet aircraft as they felt that jet aircraft were safer than aircraft with rotating propellers.

This was recognised as a problem within Saab Aircraft AB. The customer, Crossair, also saw this as a problem: 'A jet engine is economical if you fly at a high [altitude]. If you do just a [short hop], it [makes] no sense, because you never reach the flight [altitude]. You are just climbing and descending again [...]. For short routes the propeller aircraft is more efficient and more economical. But customers, they have the impression that a propeller aircraft means old technology, perhaps not as safe as a jet engine.'

Why then did the passengers' attitudes towards propeller aircraft change? One reason may be that a couple of accidents involving propeller airplanes (not Saab aircraft) occurred in the USA. These accidents resulted from a problem with ice build-up on the aircraft; the accidents had nothing to do with the fact that the planes were propeller aircraft. However, as these accidents led to loss of life, they were widely publicised and the safety of propeller aircraft was under much discussion.

As both the Saab 340 and the forthcoming Saab 2000 were propeller aircraft, they were deemed 'old-fashioned and less safe aircraft' by the passengers, even though none of the aircraft involved in the accidents had been made by Saab. Saab Aircraft AB also flew a Saab 2000 to the USA and was able to show in tests that its aircraft did not have the same ice-related problem as the ones involved in the accidents.

In summary, the new product (Saab 2000) seemed to be the right one to develop and all the parties involved agreed that the product development decision was the right one at the time when it was made. For several reasons, however, an excellent product never became a sales success. Firstly, some competitors chose to develop another type of solution – one that was more expensive for customers but suddenly became seen as 'modern'. The Saab 2000 was seen as old-fashioned by passengers already at the initiation, in part because of accidents involving a similar aircraft type. Secondly, the market for regional aircraft was limited and competition was fierce. This meant that Saab Aircraft AB made losses and could not rectify the situation, because the company's competitors could keep the prices of their aircraft at a lower level which, in the long run, was impossible for Saab Aircraft AB. The company therefore decided to terminate production of its regional aircraft even though it was seen as superior to competing products. As one of the engineers involved in development of Saab 2000 stated: '... it is the most modern aircraft on the market, seen from the technical side, but it is too expensive. [...] As a passenger I would choose [...] this aircraft over others, because I know that it is a very solid product. If you fly on a 340 or 2000, then you fly safely.'

Key points for managers

- Project termination is not necessarily as easy and natural as expected when a project is started.
- Termination is different from other phases of the project life-cycle, and calls for special skills and competences.
- When a project lasts longer, costs more and/or the quality does not meet the set criteria, the project management and senior executives should seriously consider ending the project and making the necessary termination decision.
- Project termination is difficult and the decision to do so involves many hindrances. In spite of this, wise managers, both project managers and general managers, consider project termination as a serious option in project management.
- In the case of a decision to terminate a project, it is necessary to start planning and organising a specific Ending Project.
- The Ending Project requires a well-structured planning process, in the same way as planning and execution of the initial project.

Notes

1   Sahlin-Andersson, K. and Söderholm, A. (eds) (2002) *Beyond Project Management: New Perspectives on the Temporary–Permanent Dilemma*, Liber, Abstrakt and Copenhagen Business School, p. 16.
2   Royer, I. (2005) 'Why Bad Projects Are So Hard to Kill', in *Harvard Business Review on Managing Projects*, Boston, Massachusetts: Harvard Business School Publishing Corporation, pp. 85–108. Originally published in *Harvard Business Review*, February 2003.
3   Staw, B. M. and Ross, J. (2005) 'Knowing When to Pull the Plug', in *Harvard Business Review on Managing Projects*, Massachusetts: Harvard Business School Publishing Corporation, pp. 65–84. Originally published in *Harvard Business Review*, March–April 1987, p. 66.
4   Lock, D. (2003) *Project Management*, Burlington, USA: Gower, pp. 593–606.
5   *A Guide to the Project Management Body of Knowledge: PMBOK Guide* (2004), 3rd edn, Pennsylvania, Project Management Institute, p. 5.
6   Field, M. and Keller, L. (1998) *Project Management*, Oxford: International Thomson Business Press, p. 3.
7   Lundin, R. A. and Söderholm, A. (1995) 'A Theory of the Temporary Organization', *Scandinavian Journal of Management*, 11, p. 439.
8   Ibid., p. 440.
9   See, e.g., Field and Keller, op. cit.; Meredith, J. R. and Mantel, S. J. Jr (2000) *Project Management. A Managerial Approach*, 4th edn, John Wiley & Sons; Turner J. R. (1999) *The Handbook of Project-based Management*, 2nd edn, London: McGraw-Hill.
10   Lock, op. cit., p. 16.
11   Ibid., p. 18.

12 See, e.g., Meredith and Mantel, op. cit., pp. 187–8.
13 See, e.g., ibid., pp. 307–39.
14 Ibid., p. 552.
15 See, e.g., Lock, op. cit.; Meredith and Mantel, op. cit.; Turner, op. cit.
16 Turner, op. cit., p. 329.
17 Ibid.
18 Ibid., pp. 331–2.
19 Meredith and Mantel, op. cit.
20 Lock, op. cit.
21 Turner, op. cit., p. 329.
22 Ibid., p. 330.
23 See, e.g., Meredith and Mantel, op. cit., p. 539.
24 Staw and Ross, op. cit.
25 Engwall, M. (1995) *Jakten på det effektiva projektet*, Stockholm: Thomson Fakta AB.
26 Lundin and Söderholm, op. cit., p. 449.
27 Davis, D. (2005) 'New Projects: Beware of False Economies', in *Harvard Business Review on Managing Projects*, Boston, Massachusetts: Harvard Business School Publishing Corporation, pp. 19–39. Originally published in *Harvard Business Review*, March–April 1985, p. 37.
28 Lock, op. cit., pp. 593–4.
29 Lundin and Söderholm, op. cit., p. 449.
30 Lake, C. (1998) *Mastering Project Management*, Thorogood.
31 Spirer, H. F. and Hamburger, D. H. (1988) 'Phasing Out the Project', in Cleland, D. I. and King, W. R. (eds) *Project Management Handbook*, 2nd edn, New York: Van Nostrand Reinhold, pp. 231–50.
32 Royer, op. cit.
33 Meredith and Mantel, op. cit., p. 554.

2 Network context of the project

In this chapter we shall introduce a central aspect to be considered when ending a project; namely, the network context of a project. A project is always carried out in a specific context, and these contexts differ widely, depending on the project type. Some projects have extensive contexts, meaning that they involve relations with several parties, including parties external to the company; whereas other projects are run internally and involve only (few) persons and/or units within the company itself.

This chapter has three sections: firstly, it discusses the importance of the network context for any project (Projects are open systems) and presents the extensive network context of our empirical case; secondly, shows the challenges for project termination arising from the network context (Project termination and the network context); finally, it sums up the key issues for managers.

Projects are open systems

The project management literature tends to concentrate on individual projects, omitting the project's historical and organisational context.[1] Project managers, too, are inclined to isolate their projects from outside influences, thinking that they may best make progress by focusing only on the project. This isolation may, however, be detrimental to the project. Kreiner[2] points out that developments in the environment may erode the intended project outcome, and Engwall[3] argues that the specific context of a project contains an explanation for the success or failure of a project. It is therefore crucial to take a contextual view of projects and to analyse them as open systems.

The business network approach

In this book we shall go one step further. Not only do we recognise the importance of the project context, but we also show that the project and its context are linked so intimately (especially in a termination situation) that project management in fact means management of the project context and its many different relations. For the purpose of analysing the project context, we apply the *business network approach* [4].

Project managers traditionally define the stakeholders of a project. The stakeholders may include, for instance, the project owner, the project manager, the main contractor, subcontractors, suppliers, project workers, banks, the general public, local residents and environmental groups. What is new in our perspective is not only the attention paid to stakeholders but also the consideration given to relations with stakeholders and amongst them. That is, we are interested in the connections between the company and the various stakeholders. Other connections are critical to Ending Projects as well; these are discussed in detail in Chapter 5.

According to the business network approach, any one relation between two business parties is influenced by the other relations that the two parties have. Thus, the business world is viewed as consisting of business networks of connected relations. From the viewpoint of one company, the entities to which it is connected (both directly and indirectly), and that it perceives as relevant for business, form the *network context* for its business operations.[5]

Thus, the business network approach offers a way to understand and analyse relations that are either directly or indirectly connected to a project and the companies involved in the project. As will be shown later, project stakeholders may communicate with one another directly, without going through the project team. This connection is important to understand when ending a project.

Another reason for applying the business network approach here is its focus on dynamics.[6] As we see it, when an Ending Project is being planned, it is not enough to focus only on the initial or direct stakeholders. While these may be important actors to consider when the project is being defined, initiated and run, it may well be that in project termination, different actors take on a role that is more important or radically different. The stakeholders, or rather, relations with and amongst them, therefore require special attention in project endings.

What is the network context of a project?

When applying the business network approach to a project situation, we scrutinise the various actors connected with the project both directly and indirectly through directly connected actors. These directly and indirectly connected actors are perceived as relevant from the project's point of view and constitute the network context of the project.[7] This context always differs from one project to another.

Some of the actors in the network context are more self-evident than others.

For example, in the case of internal IT system development, the project's network context comprises the units and individuals within the company, and possibly external consultants. Since the latter may use the project as a reference for their future projects, the influence of the initial project work grows. Another example of a project is a large interorganisational product development project, such as Saab Aircraft AB's development of its two aircraft types. In this situation, the network context included not only departments and individuals within the company, but also a large number of external parties such as suppliers, suppliers' suppliers, customers, passengers and the Swedish Government, to name a few.

In Box 2.1: The project network context from Saab Aircraft AB's point of view, we present the most important network actors in our real-life case on the production and delivery of the two aircraft types. The presentation illustrates the extensiveness of the network that would be directly affected by closing down the production programmes.

Box 2.1 The project network context from Saab Aircraft AB's point of view

The company, Saab Aircraft AB, co-ordinated the product development and production programmes of the two aircraft types (the Saab 340 and the Saab 2000). For the Saab 2000, Saab Aircraft AB made 15 per cent of the aircraft; the rest was obtained from different suppliers. The immediate network context included actors within the company as well as those outside it. The most important actors were the key investor (government), the employees of the company, a large number of suppliers, Saab Aircraft AB's leasing company, the aircraft operators and the company's after-sales function (maintenance services).

The Swedish Government

The Swedish Government had invested 1.5 billion Swedish crowns in risk capital for the development of the two commercial aircraft types. From the beginning, the agreement with the government was that Saab AB would repay the investment through royalties on the aircraft produced.

Saab Aircraft AB's 1,800 employees

In 1997, when the decision to cease production was made, Saab Aircraft AB had 1,800 employees whose jobs were linked with production of the two commercial aircraft types, the Saab 340 and the Saab 2000.

Both aircraft types had passed the development stage, but were at very different stages of their production life-cycles. The Saab 340 was an ongoing and successful production programme. The Saab 2000, by contrast, was in the beginning of production; only thirty airplanes had left Saab Aircraft AB's production facilities in Sweden.

For the decision-makers, it was important to take into consideration that some of the employees might leave the company soon after the decision to end production was officially announced. It was important for the company to keep the most important employees so that customers would get on-time delivery of the airplanes they had already ordered.

Saab Aircraft AB as the network co-ordinator

Saab Aircraft AB handled co-ordination of the complex production network and the interfaces between the different components purchased. Suppliers delivered around 80 per cent of the components for the Saab 340 and the Saab 2000. Saab thus interacted with suppliers actively and included them in joint planning when the aircraft was developed. Saab Aircraft AB also produced some parts. For example, the tail of the aircraft for the Saab 340 was produced by Saab Aircraft AB itself, whereas Patria Finavicomp Oy in Finland delivered the tail for the Saab 2000.

Because an aircraft is a complex and unique product that calls for huge development work and large investments, the business in this industry is characterised by co-operation within long-term relationships between the parties involved. This was expressed by one of the managers at Saab Aircraft AB as follows: 'It's not easy to change a supplier. The supplier is familiar with [...] the construction [...] and it is small series [...] This means that you have [...] a project-long relationship with the supplier. And that you must take care of that relationship, which I think we did.'

A manager at one of the supplier companies sees the relationship with Saab Aircraft AB and the other suppliers in a similar way: 'I believe Saab was among the first to introduce a networking model and used it to handle the job well [...]. Now we are partners and try to make good use of each other, and not just in a one-sided manner.' In this business, the initial choice of suppliers is therefore crucial, since the two parties are tightly bound to a long-term relationship requiring adaptation on both sides.

Normally a supplier relationship begins when the development work is launched, which means that suppliers invest in both product development and development of the tools needed for production. The relationship continues as long as the airplane is flying, which usually means a period of twenty-five to thirty years.

One reason for the long-term relationships in this industry is that it is not cost effective to change from one supplier to another once development work has started. Another reason is that steady supplier relationships make it possible to share the risks entailed in large development projects between several companies. This also means that investments for tools are divided between several parties.

Around 230 suppliers

In 1997, the number of suppliers was about 230. All of them had been involved in the projects to develop the two aircraft types, and they also became important actors in the Ending Project.

Ten to fifteen of the 230 suppliers turn out about 80 per cent of the value of the purchased components. Supply is therefore highly concentrated. About half of the suppliers are the same for both aircraft types, while around 25 per cent were suppliers only for the Saab 340 and around 25 per cent only for the Saab 2000. One of the managers at Saab Aircraft AB pointed out that the 'business relationships are about the same for the two projects, because our goal was to have the same supplier base'.

Aircraft production is global in nature and involves international business relations. Most of the suppliers were located in the USA, several in England, some in France, a few in Germany, and one in Spain. One of the managers at a supplier company explained that the suppliers knew each other fairly well 'because in our business – it is very small – and you meet people at air shows etc.' and continued that 'we knew other people who were supplying for the Saab 2000 and 340'.

In the beginning of the development projects for the Saab 340 and the Saab 2000, some of the suppliers were in contact with each other. But once all the initial product development problems had been solved, the various suppliers were not directly in touch with one another. One of the suppliers illustrates this as follows: 'I don't very often speak to the wheel and brake manufacturer because the interface between the wheel and the brake and the landing gear is a Saab responsibility [...] So once you get it right [...] then the wheel is not an issue.'

Thus, even though the suppliers did not communicate with each other on a daily basis, most of them knew each other and, as needed, could communicate both through Saab Aircraft AB and directly.

Aircraft leasing

Early in the commercial aircraft production programme, Saab Aircraft AB started leasing of the aircraft. Most regional airlines lacked the creditworthiness to purchase their aircraft, which meant that leasing from Saab was the only way the aircraft could be placed with regional operators. Operators paid a monthly rent that was usually 1–1.5 per cent of the original selling price of the aircraft.

At the end of the 1990s, Saab Aircraft Leasing AB was the world leader in leasing aircraft to regional operators. In 1999 the company had an organisation consisting of twenty persons in Sweden, twenty in Washington, five in Australia and one in Tokyo. Around 5–10 per cent of the aircraft in the lease portfolio were returned every year. This means that each year, between fifteen and thirty aircraft had to be placed with new operators. Saab Aircraft Leasing AB had been successful in leasing its fleet; in September 1999, only seven aircraft out of the total fleet of over 500 aircraft were on the ground.

At their original delivery, most of the aircraft were leased to regional operators for long lease periods, approximately fifteen years. As each operator has its own colours and logos, an airplane returned after a lease has to be repainted before it can be leased out again. From the customer's point of view, there is little difference whether the aircraft is brand new or has been in use, as the parts of an aircraft are changed continuously. As the Managing Director of Saab Aircraft Leasing AB put it: 'A ten-year-old aircraft is as good as one that is only one or five or three years old.'

In September 1998, Saab Aircraft Leasing AB had a leasing portfolio consisting in total of 310 aircraft. Of these, 280 were Saab 340 planes and thirty were Saab 2000 planes. The value of this portfolio was 11 billion Swedish crowns. It was therefore important to lease out the aircraft as soon as they came back from one operator. As one of the managers at Saab Aircraft AB pointed out: 'During the termination, the financial commitments represented by the fleet were among the company's big worries. How would we take care of the value of this fleet? How could we ensure the value of the portfolio?'

Crossair: the launching partner and an important customer

One important actor in the network was Crossair, which had been the launching partner for the Saab 340 and continued as the launching partner also for 'the 340's bigger sister, the Saab 2000'. Therefore, it played an active role in determining the specifications of the aircraft, too.

The prototype of the Saab 2000 was ready at the end of 1991, and was presented to Crossair at a gala ceremony on 14 December 1991, with the King and Queen of Sweden in attendance. In 1999, Crossair had bought twelve Saab 340 aircraft and thirty-four Saab 2000 aircraft.

During the first five years after a new aircraft has been launched, it is still under development. This meant regular contacts between Saab Aircraft AB, several of the suppliers and airlines operating the aircraft. In the beginning of 1997, the Saab 2000 had just passed these first five years of development.

Around seventy airlines operating Saab aircraft

Many of the airlines that started to use the Saab 340 in 1982–83 continued to use Saab aircraft. In 1999, some seventy airlines around the world were operating the Saab 340 and/or the Saab 2000.

The USA was the largest market, and here Saab also had a subsidiary for customer support. In the USA, American Eagle had the biggest Saab fleet, consisting of 115 Saab 340 aircraft. In Europe, Crossair had the biggest Saab fleet. The customers outside the USA were smaller, anywhere from two to fifteen aircraft. All of the operators flying the Saab 340 and the Saab 2000 in Europe and North America were connected to bigger airlines that flew longer routes.

To illustrate, Table 2.1 lists the operators that were flying the Saab 340 aircraft in 1999. As the table shows, forty-one operators used the Saab 340 in 1999 and most of the aircraft were located in the USA.

Table 2.1 Saab 340 operators in 1999.

Name of operator	Country	Number of aircraft
American Eagle	USA	115
Mesaba Airlines	USA	73
Business Express	USA	39
Express Airlines I	USA	34
Kendell Airlines	Australia	16
Chautauqua	USA	14
Air Nelson	New Zealand	13
Crossair	Switzerland	12

Name of operator	*Country*	*Number of aircraft*
Japan Air Commuter	Japan	11
Skyways AB	Sweden	10
British Midland	Great Britain	9
Hazelton Airlines	Australia	8
Shandong Airlines	China	8
Swedish Air Force	Sweden	7
Aerolitoral	Mexico	6
Air Botnia	Finland	5
Calm Air	Canada	4
Flying Enterprise	Sweden	4
Golden Air	Sweden	4
Air Ostrava	Czech Republic	3
Hokkaido Air Systems	Japan	3
Kaiken Lineas Aereas	Argentina	3
Aurigny Air Services	Great Britain	2
Crossair Europe	France	2
Finnair Prop	Finland	2
Formosa Airlines	Taiwan	2
Japan Maritime Safety Agency	Japan	2
Lithuanian Airlines	Lithuania	2
Loganair	Great Britain	2
Macair	Australia	2
Peninsula Airways	USA	2
Regional Airlines	France	2
TAN	Argentina	2
Kelly Springfield	USA	1
Light Air	USA	1
Mellon Bank	USA	1
Moldavian Airlines	Moldavian Rep	1
Ostfriesische Lufttransport	Germany	1
Raslan Air Service	Egypt	1
Tapsa	Argentina	1
Slovak Airlines	Slovakia	1

Source Saab Aircraft Leasing Market Report, Issue 7, September 1999.

Table 2.2, in turn, lists the operators that used the Saab 2000 in 1999. As this table shows, nine operators flew the Saab 2000. Only three of these operators (Crossair of Switzerland, Regional Airlines of France, and Lithuanian Airlines of Lithuania, indicated in the table in *italics*) flew both aircraft types.

Table 2.2 Saab 2000 operators in 1999.

Name of operator	Country	Number of aircraft
Crossair	Switzerland	34
Regional Airlines	France	8
SAS Commuter	Sweden	6
GMWTS	USA	3
CityJet	Ireland	2
Japan Civil Aviation Bureau	Japan	2
Lithuanian Airlines	Lithuania	2
Med Airlines	Italy	2
Air Marshall Islands	Marshall Islands	1

Source Saab Aircraft Leasing Market Report, Issue 7, September 1999.

Customer support

A specific feature of the industry is that the aircraft producer needs to ensure spare parts and maintenance service for around twenty-five years after the product is taken into use. In addition, the producer must be able to continue to develop the aircraft. The authorities may require changes, such as new systems and functions for the aircraft. Or changes may be needed, for instance, due to new technology – as with the development of communications – or in order to increase passenger comfort onboard by means of new service and catering arrangements.

This means that to be able to keep the 'aircraft flying', Saab AB needed to convince the operators that they would have the capacity and capabilities to sell spare parts and provide the necessary needed maintenance in future, and would also be able to continue to develop the existing fleet.

The description set out in Box 2.1 illustrates the challenging and complex context in which the Ending Project was realised. In particular, it shows how important it was to convince customers (operators) that there would be a continuing supply of spare parts and maintenance and the preconditions for maintaining the required relations with suppliers. In addition, there were relations with several other stakeholders that needed to be managed well during project termination.

Next we discuss the basis for analysis of the project network context, i.e. the key aspects managers must understand are necessary in order to manage the project network context.

The network context of a project is always unique

Each project has a unique network context. We illustrate this in Figure 2.1 by looking at two projects and their specific stakeholders. The reason for this uniqueness is threefold: the stakeholders, the relationships and the connections between the relations all vary.

Firstly, both the number and the characteristics of the stakeholders involved in the project always vary from one project to another. Figure 2.1 illustrates this as follows: Project A has three direct stakeholders (A.1, A.2 and A.3). Of these stakeholders, A.3 is more important for the project than the other two. This is indicated by the larger circle in the figure. Project B, in turn, illustrates a totally different type of project network context, as there are seven direct stakeholders of equal importance.

Another factor that makes each project network context unique is the differences in relations amongst the parties involved. Figure 2.1 illustrates this by variations in the thickness of the connecting lines. For example, in Project A, stakeholder A.3 has a more extensive relationship to the project than stakeholders A.1 and A.2. Such a situation might be the case, for instance, if more individuals representing stakeholder A.3 were involved in the project in several different ways. Similarly, there is variation in the stakeholders' relations in Project B, despite the relatively similar importance of the stakeholders *per se.*

A third reason for the uniqueness of each project's network context is the type of connectedness of the relations. In Figure 2.1, stakeholder A.3 has two suppliers connected with Project A through the stakeholder, which thus become indirect stakeholders. Furthermore, stakeholder A.2 and stakeholder A.3 are also directly connected to each other, which might reflect, for instance, some sort of co-operation between these two stakeholders. Project B, in turn, illustrates a situation where the seven stakeholders are connected to each other only through the project. Project B illustrates an extreme situation, as there are usually some connections between at least some of the stakeholders.

While the existing project management literature stresses the task of identifying the number and type of stakeholders having an interest in a project,[8] it fails to explore the connections. Especially in a project-ending situation,

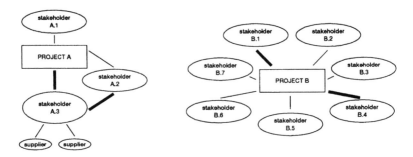

Figure 2.1 Different project network contexts.

however, it becomes crucial to identify not only the relevant stakeholders but also the *type of relations* and the *direct and indirect connections* existing between the different parties. Thus, in this book we highlight the importance of recognising all actors that may be affected by termination of the project, or alternatively, that may influence the termination process.

Project termination and the network context

The strength of the business network approach is that it has advanced our understanding of dynamics in business relationships as well as our understanding of how changes in one individual business relationship may influence other business relationships.[9] This knowledge is important when terminating a project, as termination means that different relations with the project's stakeholders are terminated or changed.

Termination of individual business relationships

Researchers have traditionally been interested in how to develop and maintain business relationships. The early progress made in the area focused on development processes in business relationships. Relationships were seen as going through different phases or stages, with one of these phases being the ending phase.[10]

However, it was not until at the end of the 1990s that endings of business relationships, in particular, began attracting researchers' interest.[11] Today we know that the ending situations of business relationships can differ widely. The different ending situations have been characterised, for instance, as follows: dissolution; termination; exit; switching behaviour; and fading. Indeed, business relationships may be ended under very different conditions and for very different reasons. Research shows that the process of relationship dissolution may be a complex and complicated process that disconnects the two business parties from each other; or it may be a natural process based on mutual agreement, where the possibilities for future business are retained. Much depends on the managers involved and their skills in relationship termination.

When terminating a business relationship, managers need to understand the particular characteristics of the relationship in question. According to the network approach, every business relationship is unique, due, for instance, to the developments that have taken place over time and the parties' experiences of one another.[12] These past developments also affect how the parties see, and react to, the project ending.

In our empirical case, these historic backgrounds became evident, for instance, in the negotiations conducted between the company and the suppliers during the project termination phase. Not surprisingly, the suppliers were affected by their view of past developments, and so the background of the relationship influenced the negotiations. But the suppliers considered not only the past developments in the relationship as such, but also what had happened in their other relationships (with other customers) (see Box 2.2: History matters). Suppliers who felt that the interaction atmosphere and previous history had been positive seemed to have a wider acceptance for changes, even dramatic ones.

Box 2.2 History matters

Whether the negotiation process in the termination phase progressed smoothly or not seemed to depend on the past history of relationships between Saab Aircraft AB and the suppliers. This was expressed as follows by one of the managers at Saab Aircraft AB: 'The process went well with those suppliers with whom we have had a good relationship and that we have taken good care of. Those we have been rough with, when we haven't had the right continuity in contacts, a change of personnel on our side and the supplier side, where there has not been a co-operative atmosphere – it is these suppliers that appeared to be troublesome now.'

In one case, the supplier had had negative experiences in other, prior relationships that had involved financial loss. This supplier was now extra careful, and did not want to deliver before they received payment for what had been delivered earlier. During a short period in the beginning of 1998, it went so far that a halt in delivery took place. The parties reached an agreement, however, and the future deliveries

> of spare parts were secured. One of the managers at Saab Aircraft AB stated: 'They were cautious [...]. As soon as anything about closing down was mentioned, they wanted payment in advance for everything [...] that had been delivered [...]. Then they investigated our business and learnt that so far, the company's solidity wasn't especially weak [...] so it was not a problem.'

The uniqueness of business relationships means that during the Ending Project, each relation should, to a certain degree, be handled in its own unique way. Of course, not all project endings mean that individual business relationships are ended. But when this is the case, it is important to understand that an individual relationship is always connected to other relationships, and that the impacts of project termination may spread far in the network context of the project.[13]

Management of unique, parallel and interconnected relations in project termination

The main difference between terminating a business relationship and terminating a project is the complexity arising from the number of parties involved. Several individuals from each of the parties may be involved in a business relationship, but they still represent one of the two parties. Projects, in turn, usually involve more than two parties. Even projects that are internal to the company may involve representatives (individuals) from different departments or functions of the company. Other, external projects involve individuals representing several different companies.

In an ending situation, the complexity of the project is a challenge for managers, as they need to manage termination processes at two levels: firstly, the manager needs to handle each individual relationship and secondly, the manager needs to address the connections between these. In consequence, managers terminating complex projects often need to handle several interconnected relationships with various actors simultaneously.

In Box 2.3: Different supplier relationships in the network context, we illustrate the complexities that a manager may encounter when planning an Ending Project. We use supplier relationships as an example, and thus show how even one stakeholder group of a project – suppliers – may include very different partners and relationships. This example illustrates that each relation is unique. It also shows that it was clear from the beginning of the Ending Project that the changes expected in the supplier relationships heavily depended on the type of products that were delivered. Some supplier relationships would need to be terminated, while others were only expected to change in nature.

For these reasons, management of project termination is not merely a job for planners and schedulers; the general management of the company/companies involved should also take part. It is not enough for a key account manager, who is responsible for a customer/supplier relationship, to decide on termination of a relationship without considering the impacts of termination and its connections to the company's other relationships; correspondingly, it is not sufficient to leave the termination of a project to the project manager if the termination may affect the company network widely. Very often, project termination needs to be planned at the strategic level.

Box 2.3 Different supplier relationships in the network context

In 1999, when the last aircraft was produced, Saab Aircraft AB knew that it would be involved in this business until around 2025–30, or as long as the aircraft were in traffic. The situation was similar for the suppliers that needed to produce spare parts for the aircraft. As one of the managers at Saab Aircraft AB said, this meant that '… at the same time one needs to consider that we are going to have a relationship with this supplier afterwards, also regarding after-sales market'. He continued: 'This may mean that in some cases it will cost some dollars more than we had thought, but it is an investment in future relations, as they will last at least twenty years.'

Structural parts in the aircraft

Among the 230 suppliers, those supplying structural parts would suffer considerably from termination of the production. The structural parts of an aircraft are specific to each aircraft type, which means that the suppliers of these parts had invested in product development. One outcome of ending production would be a clear drop in demand for their products, also because in most cases, these products require very few spare parts.

The biggest structural part of the Saab 2000 is the wing, which was supplied by CASA Construcciones Aeronauticas S. A. in Spain. Other structural parts of the Saab 2000 include the tail supplied by Patria Finavicomp Oy in Finland, and the rear fuselage supplied by Westland in England.

Moving parts in an aircraft

Suppliers who manufacture moving parts in an aircraft will continue to deliver spare parts in the same way as during the production phase. This was expressed by one of the managers at Saab Aircraft AB as follows: 'When an airplane shows wear, replacement parts are needed, especially the engine [...]. You can calculate fairly precisely in dollars per flying hour, for which you usually can sell spare parts. So they were facing a long flow of income. But the suppliers of fuselage did not have that.' Thus, the situation for suppliers of moving parts was not as serious as that for companies supplying structural parts.

Other examples of moving parts that are needed continuously are propellers, brakes and wheels. These supplies would probably not be problematic when ending the production, as the relationship with their suppliers would not change in the short run.

Aircraft-specific parts

Another reason that suppliers of moving parts normally would not suffer as much from the termination of production as suppliers of structural parts was that their products are used also in other aircraft, and were thus not developed specifically for the Saab 340 or the Saab 2000. As one of the managers at a supplier company pointed out: 'An engine manufacturer uses a different kind of logic in this matter [...]. Allison did not end up in exactly the same situation, as its engine is used in many other airplanes today. It did not mean the end of the project for Allison; it only lost one part of the project'. He continued that the situation was different for suppliers of parts that are aircraft specific: 'Nobody else needs such things. These parts were not suitable for anything else.'

The landing gear, supplied by APPH Ltd in the UK, is an example of a product that is specific for each aircraft. APPH Ltd specialises in designing and manufacturing landing gear systems for regional aircraft. The company designed, certified and manufactured the landing gear for both the Saab 340 and the Saab 2000.

Supplier to the Saab 340 or the Saab 2000 – or both?

There was also a difference depending on whether the supplier supplied to the Saab 340 or the Saab 2000. As a manager at a company supplying for the Saab 340 stated: 'So being left with stock was not a problem because when you have 400 aeroplanes flying, they need spares. Everything that we had was useful and useable in the short term as well as in the long term.'

However, even though it was a question of spare parts that were needed continuously, if the supplier only supplied to the Saab 2000, termination of production would mean a reduced prospect of future sales, as only sixty-three aircraft were built. The problem for these suppliers was not only the small number of aircraft but also that the aircraft was new, which meant a reduced need for maintenance.

Saab Aircraft AB was aware of this situation, which was expressed by one of the managers as follows: 'Those who are [supplying to] the 340 have nothing to complain about, as there are 450 airplanes [in use]. Those who are only involved with the Saab 2000 think that it is bad, or a thin base for future deliveries of spare parts.'

Saab, a small customer?

Suppliers of components to aircraft do not normally have more than 3–5 per cent of their sales going to one customer, which means that in most cases they will not suffer dramatically when one contract is brought to an end. Only in some cases is the percentage as high as 15–20 per cent. As the production was not terminated overnight, many of the suppliers had time to adapt to the new situation. Some suppliers, however, were forced to shrink their business when Saab Aircraft AB terminated contracts pertaining to the Saab 340 and the Saab 2000.

To conclude our discussion on relationship termination and project endings in a network context, we need to address the question of how to conduct network analysis around a project. In this book, we describe the project network context and its developments for one empirical case example. These analytic illustrations are based on the information collected from different parties in the network context, thus making analysis of the network context of the project (especially with regard to developments in ending, to be discussed later) more 'objective', in the sense that we have relied on multiple sources of information. Our view of the project network context is, on the one hand, more extensive, but on the other, much more superficial than the view of the actors' actually involved in this business network.

Any individual company always perceives the network context of a project from its own position; so does each manager. While it is possible for managers (for the purposes of strategic evaluation) to pinpoint key actors, and especially the direct relations involved, the indirect connections are much more difficult to perceive. This aspect will be further discussed in Chapter 5, where we discuss the identification of different connections. Another issue is that the closer one comes to the evaluation of individual relationships, the more relevant information can be obtained from those people actively involved in these interactions.

Thus, for any company to construct the network contexts of its projects (or indeed, of the company itself), a key tool would be to collect information from different levels, functions and people within the company. Business relationships and networks can only be superficially investigated from outside – insider involvement and perceptions are the key to their understanding. Moreover, to understand the present state or potential future developments of the business relationships, one needs to understand earlier developments and the histories of relationship. Thus, to construct an understanding of the network context of a project, a wise project manager is open to information from both strategic and operational levels of the company and from all individuals who have been involved in the project, and actively seeks such information.

Key points for managers

- A network view of the project directs attention not only to project stakeholders, but rather to the relations with them and amongst them, and also considers indirect relations.
- The network context of a project includes actors who are relevant from the point of view of the project and who are connected both directly and indirectly.
- Each project has a unique network context.
- Managers need to pay attention to the individual relations in the project context, as each relation has its own special features and thus needs to be handled in a unique way in project termination.
- It is important to recognise all actors who may be affected by project termination, or alternatively, who may influence the termination process.
- A key managerial challenge in project termination is the management of unique, parallel and interconnected relations.

Notes

1 Recently, the project context has attracted increasing interest from researchers (see, for instance, Sahlin-Andersson, K. and Söderholm, A. (eds) (2002) *Beyond Project Management: New Perspectives on the Temporary–Permanent Dilemma*,

Liber, Abstrakt and Copenhagen Business School). These approaches, however, are different from the network context of projects that is advanced here.
2 Kreiner, K. (1995) 'In Search of Relevance: Project Management in Drifting Environments', *Scandinavian Journal of Management*, 11, 335–46.
3 Engwall, M. (2003) 'No Project Is an Island: Linking Projects to History and Context', *Research Policy*, 32, 789–808.
4 See, e.g., Anderson, J. C., Håkansson, H. and Johanson, J. (1994) 'Dyadic Business Relationships within a Business Network Context', *Journal of Marketing*, 58, 1–15; Ford, D. (1998) *Managing Business Relationships*, Chichester, UK: Wiley; Håkansson, H. and Snehota, I. (1989) 'No Business Is an Island: The Network Concept of Business Strategy', *Scandinavian Journal of Management*, 22, 256–70; Håkansson, H. and Snehota, I. (eds) (1995) *Developing Relationships in Business Networks*, London: Routledge.
5 Anderson, Håkansson and Johanson, op. cit.; Håkansson and Snehota, 1989, op. cit.
6 See, for instance, Halinen, A., Salmi, A. and Havila, V. (1999) 'From Dyadic Change to Changing Business Networks: An Analytical Framework', *Journal of Management Studies*, 36, 779–94.
7 Researchers in the area have proposed also the concept of 'milieu' in project marketing, consisting of a territory, a network of actors, a common representation of business and a set of tacit rules (see, Cova, B., Mazet, F. and Salle, R. (1996) 'Milieu as a Pertinent Unit of Analysis in Project Marketing', *International Business Review*, 5, 647–64). The difference to our 'network context of a project' is that 'milieu' is seen to be geographically bound, whereas the boundaries around the 'network context of a project' is defined by the relevance for the project. The tacit rules, in turn, we find to be important also in the network context. In particular, the ending processes in projects are tightly linked to the norms and rules that have been formed earlier.
8 See, e.g., Lock, D. (2003) *Project Management*, Burlington, USA: Gower, pp. 13–15.
9 See, for instance, Halinen *et al.*, op. cit.; Håkansson and Snehota, 1995, op. cit.
10 Dwyer, F. R., Schurr, P. H. and Oh, S. (1987) 'Developing Buyer–Seller Relationships', *Journal of Marketing*, 51, 11–27; Ford, D. (1980) 'The Development of Buyer–Seller Relationships in Industrial Markets', *European Journal of Marketing*, 14, 339–53.
11 There is a stream of contemporary research focusing on business relationship ending and dissolution. Examples include: Alajoutsijärvi, K., Möller, K. and Tähtinen, J. (2000) 'Beautiful Exit: How to Leave Your Business Partner', *European Journal of Marketing*, 34, 1270–90; Giller, C. and Matear, S. (2001) 'The Termination of Inter-firm Relationships', *The Journal of Business & Industrial Marketing*, 16, 94–112; Halinen, A. and Tähtinen J. (2002) 'A Process Theory of Relationship Ending', *International Journal of Service Industry Management*, 13, 163–80; Harrison, D. (2004) 'Is a Long-term Business Relationship an Implied Contract? Two Views of Relationship Disengagement', *Journal of Management Studies*, 41, 107–25; Havila, V. and Wilkinson, I. (2002) 'The Principle of the Conservation of Relationship Energy: or Many Kinds of New Beginnings', *Industrial Marketing Management*, 31, 191–203; Holmlund-Rytkönen, M. and Strandvik, T. (2005) 'Stress in Business Relationships', *Journal of Business & Industrial Marketing*, 20, 12–22; Pressey, A. D. and Mathews, B. P. (2003) 'Jumped, Pushed or Forgotten? Approaches to Dissolution', *Journal of Marketing Management*, 19, 131–55; Tähtinen, J.

(2001) 'The Dissolution Process of a Business Relationship: A Case Study from Tailored Software Business', doctoral dissertation, Acta Universitatis Ouluensis G. Oeconomica 10. Oulu; Tähtinen, J. and Halinen, A. (2002) 'Research on Ending Exchange Relationships: A Categorization, Assessment and Outlook', *Marketing Theory*, 2, 165–88.

12 See, for instance, Håkansson and Snehota, 1995, op. cit.
13 Earlier research on the effects of the terminated relationship on indirectly related parties is scarce. Examples Include: Dahlin, P. (2007) 'Turbulence in Business Networks: A Longitudinal Study of Mergers, Acquisitions and Bankruptcies Involving Swedish IT Companies', doctoral dissertation, No. 53, Mälardalen University, Sweden; Havila, V. and Salmi, A. (2000) 'Spread of Change in Business Networks: An Empirical Study of Mergers and Acquisitions in the Graphics Industry', *Journal of Strategic Marketing*, 8, 105–19.

3   Project-ending strategy

A project-ending strategy is needed to tackle the challenges of project termination. In this chapter we shall briefly describe the key issues that the project-ending strategy should take into account.

This chapter consists of five sections. The first (Why is a project-ending strategy needed?) addresses the need to build a strategy rather than simply allowing the project to end itself. The second (Key elements of the project-ending strategy) presents the first preparation phase of the strategy work. The third (Realisation of the need to end a project) discusses the difficulties that managers may encounter in making the final termination decision. The fourth (Planning of the Ending Project) focuses on planning of the ending strategy. This chapter thus paves the way for the Chapters 4 and 5, which examine in greater detail what is needed when implementing the ending strategy. The final section summarises the key points for managers.

Why is a project-ending strategy needed?

Projects that keep to their deadline and budget and reach their goals (at least within accepted limits) are not difficult to end. In such a situation the ending is uncomplicated and follows the planned trajectory naturally. Reporting and evaluation are crucial ending tasks, but no specific ending strategy is needed; the plan made during the initiation phase suffices.

However, when a project lasts longer, costs more and/or the quality does not meet the criteria set, it becomes important to plan for its ending. Similarly, when a project needs to be terminated earlier than had been scheduled, special attention should be paid to the planning of its ending. In these cases, the strategic skills of the company and project managers are weighed. Careful planning is especially important if the ending is expected to affect individuals and companies outside the project team. Indeed, the ending may affect the stakeholders in various ways, and their reactions to the termination may differ from those which the project team would expect.

The goal of the ending strategy is to terminate the project in a successful way. Often this would mean limiting the cost overrun, thus improving the finances of the company. Other outcomes of success are satisfied stakeholders and an intact company image, both of which provide a basis for future business opportunities. Despite these potential benefits of an efficient ending strategy, it is difficult, as discussed in Chapter 1, to make the decision to end a project. Still, project termination is the only wise decision to make more often than is realised. And careful planning is essential to ensure that project termination is successful.

Key elements of the project-ending strategy

The strategic work on project ending begins when the company first realises the potential need to end the project, and it comes to a close when the project has been terminated and the ending has been evaluated within the company. The termination process thus involves the following elements:

1   Realisation of the need to end a project
2   Planning of the Ending Project
3   Execution of the Ending Project.

The first issue, realisation of the need to end a project, is a real challenge for managers. As discussed in Chapter 1, a myriad of reasons may cause the need to end a project in a way or at a time that is different from what had initially been planned. Much sensitivity and attention are required of managers, at different levels, to give right interpretations to the various signals indicating the need for project ending. To orientate towards ending is tricky, given that projects typically exceed their timelines or costs to at least some extent.

Therefore, the relevant question for managers to consider is: When can one follow the original project plan and when is a specific ending strategy for the project needed? The empirical example illustrated that the network context of the project was extensive and that many stakeholders, including the central case firm, had invested heavily in the aircraft production programmes. It was therefore a challenge to start considering termination. Yet despite the difficulties, the general management took this option seriously and launched the necessary preparations.

Planning for the ending is critical for a successful Ending Project. The important actors are identified and a plan is drawn up specifying how and when they should be approached. It is also important to decide who will address the different actors. These (strategic) decisions should be taken above the project manager, at the general management level of the company, and they should involve several functions of the company.

Execution of the Ending Project involves several parties: the initial project team, the ending project team, and other project stakeholders. The success of ending essentially depends on how well the different parties can be motivated in the termination situation.

Project plans usually end with evaluation, and some evaluation should also take place in Ending Projects. Evaluation of the ending process increases the potential for learning[1] and for developing the company's ending competences for future needs. As we see it, an on-going evaluation should be an integral part of the termination process. Therefore, evaluation is not discussed separately, but is taken as one element of ending competences. These are discussed in Chapter 4, which focuses on the Ending Project execution.

In this chapter we shall take a closer look at the first two parts of a project termination strategy: realisation of the need to end a project and planning of the Ending Project.

Realisation of the need to end a project

The ending strategy starts with the realisation that the project should be terminated and, consequently, that a specific project-ending strategy should be drawn up. This calls for analytical skills and visionary thinking at the general management level. The decision to end a project cannot be made by the project manager. Instead, this decision must be taken at the level of the superiors. In the case of extensive projects, this means the general management level or the Board of Directors. But even at this level it is, as Davis notes, 'a brave manager who recommends the abandonment of a project'[2].

Indeed, the general managers are needed because, firstly, they have the power to make radical decisions and to redirect the company, and secondly, because they are the ones responsible for the company's strategies and long-term developments. Thus, they are able to overcome the problems and hindrances arising from the project termination decision.

Before making the strategic decision to end a project in a way other than had been initially planned, the general management needs to consider the following questions:

* How serious is the time-overrun?
* How serious is the problem with quality?
* How serious is the cost-overrun?

If the management has enough evidence indicating that the project has serious problems that cannot be solved, the next step is to make a deliberate decision to terminate the project and to start planning an *Ending Project*.

In our example case, the decision to end production was made by the Board of Directors of the company. The decision was easy to make because the company had tried everything in its power to correct the situation and avert the ending of the production. This is illustrated in Box 3.1: There is only one possible solution.

Box 3.1 There is only one possible solution

The decision to end production

During summer 1997 the management of Saab AB started to discuss whether the company was in fact facing a situation that would perhaps force it to discontinue the production of regional aircraft. The results of an analysis done in spring 1997 were so stark that the decision process was short. This was expressed as follows by the managing director of Saab Aircraft AB: 'It was in fact very easy to come to the conclusion that it is impossible for Saab to continue in this business, with development and construction of civil aircraft. It was so apparent that it never became an issue for discussions in itself.'

The situation regarding the Saab 340 was not as difficult as that of the Saab 2000, but to produce only one type of aircraft would not have been possible since the thinking had been that all of the costs would be borne by the production of two aircraft types.

The decision to terminate production of the Saab 340 and the Saab 2000 was taken by the Board of Directors of Saab AB in August 1997.

The planning of an Ending Project is discussed presently, but let us first examine the period before the decision to terminate a project is taken, which is often a critical period.

What hinders the ending decision?

Several factors may prevent the management from making the decision to end a project. Staw and Ross note that these factors may be psychological, social, and/or organisational.[3] They point out that when the project managers encounter an expected problem, they may see it as a sign that everything is proceeding as planned in advance and therefore they do not question the need for extra investments arising from the problem. One reason for this may be that the literature dealing with project management[4] recommends that to be able to react rapidly, a project manager should always expect a failure.

The project management may also feel that strong leadership means continuing an effort once it has been started.[5] Thus, for instance, there is a tendency to interpret the incoming information in a more positive way than would otherwise be the case. The same thinking may also hold for those who should take the actual project termination decision, especially if they where the ones who initiated the project.

High closing costs are another factor that, according to Staw and Ross,[6] hinders a project termination decision. In complex projects, the ending costs may be high and the termination itself may involve much extra work. In the case of a project that already has cost more than planned, it may be difficult to accept that the project will cost even more. But if the problems are serious enough, it is easier to decide to terminate the project, as it is obvious that termination is the best solution.

All these factors reveal the central challenge: How are the factors that may hinder the management from making the correct, fundamental decision overcome? The hindering factors are overcome by decision-making at the general management level, by careful planning and by adopting a strategic approach to project management.

Gaining advance support for the difficult decision

Before the decision to terminate a project is taken, the general management must conduct a proper analysis and – critically – must approach the relevant stakeholders so that it becomes clear to everyone that the only feasible action is termination of the project.

In the case of large and important projects, the stakeholders may need to be informed and involved even before the decision to end a project is made. Some of them may need all extra time they can get to be able to adapt smoothly to the new situation. Notification of the relevant parties before the termination decision is taken also helps to prevent the spread of incorrect and often negative rumours.

In our example case, the most important parties were notified several months before the official announcement was made on 15 December 1997. Advance notification served to prepare the general management at the most significant companies for the possibility that project termination might be the only possible course of action. As can been seen in the example case (Box 3.2: Can we avoid ending?), Saab Aircraft AB chose to involve the general management levels at the most significant companies when trying to avert project ending. Thus the most important parties had a chance to influence the situation (by lowering their prices). They also received information directly from the managing director and the three managers of the Purchasing Department at Saab Aircraft AB, which indicated that the company considered the situation from the stakeholders' viewpoint, too.

Box 3.2 Can we avoid ending?

A consultant company gives advice

One way for Saab Aircraft AB to stay in the aircraft business would have been to lower production costs. For this reason, Saab Aircraft AB contacted a consultant company that had been involved when two other aircraft manufacturers had ceased production of their turboprop aircraft (the Dornier 328 project and the Fokker 50 project). The consultant company had a database that contained information, for example, on how much each kilo of aircraft structure should cost. This information was based on the other two aircraft manufacturers' costs. The consultant company believed that it would be possible to cut costs by 30 per cent.

The 'cost-reduction campaign' during spring 1997

During spring 1997 a 'cost-reduction campaign' took place, with the aim being to lower production costs, as the price of the Saab 2000, in particular, was too high to be attractive for potential customers. This was seen as the final possible way of continuing with the production of commercial aircraft. As expressed by one of the managers at Saab Aircraft AB: '... this was the last hope that might save the project, which at that time had large profitability problems.'

Before the campaign started, Saab Aircraft AB had lowered its own costs of producing the Saab 340 by 24 per cent and those for the Saab 2000 by 27 per cent. One of the managers at Saab Aircraft AB pointed out that '... it was important to show that we had done more than we wanted the suppliers to do. We couldn't present our problem and leave its resolution to suppliers.'

The 'cost-reduction campaign' started in January 1997 and its completion was planned for June 1997. It involved the ten to fifteen largest suppliers. If these largest suppliers were unable to lower their prices, it would not matter whether the smaller suppliers would do so. Thus, the latter were not contacted at all at this stage.

The goal was that the suppliers would lower their prices by 17 per cent for the Saab 340 and by 19 per cent for the Saab 2000. And, that this price reduction would take effect more or less immediately. The main message to these suppliers was that the success of this 'cost-reduction campaign' was critical to the future of Saab's commercial aircraft production, and thus also critical to the suppliers with regard to both future orders and the possibility of recouping their investment costs. Success would mean that Saab Aircraft AB would have a competitive price for the aircraft and would thus be able to maintain or even increase the production volume.

Meeting the most important suppliers

The 'cost-reduction campaign' included both 'partner conferences' and visits to the suppliers. The reason for these conferences was to communicate with the suppliers and give information about the situation at hand.

The 'partner conferences' took place during March, April and May 1997, with a few suppliers being invited at a time. The conferences were held in Washington and London. One conference was arranged in Reno, Nevada, in April because that was the site of a fair and many important decision-makers would attend the conference.

The 'partner conferences' started with a presentation that gave the suppliers a comprehensive picture of the situation. One of the managers at Saab Aircraft AB noted that 'It was important to inform the suppliers, who we saw as partners, that our situation was troubling, that something had to be done, and that they had an important role to play when it came to the survival of the project.'

The main aim, i.e. to make the suppliers realise how serious the situation was, seemed to be achieved. According to one of the main suppliers: 'These were also beginning to be occasions that clearly indicated the direction in which we were headed.'

The sharing of information was open; the company disclosed, for example, the financial performance of Saab Aircraft AB over the years. Saab Aircraft AB saw the suppliers as partners and had a non-disclosure agreement with them; therefore the books could be shown openly.

The presentations, given in part by people of management level, included the following main areas:

* the difficult market situation, which had led to increasing price concessions due to overcapacity on the market – the market prices for regional aircraft had been declining by 3 per cent per year since January 1990;

- the fact that the future would not be better with regard to overcapacity, as there were five manufacturers and aircraft for fewer than 100 passengers accounted for only 6 per cent of the total market;
- the costs of purchased materials had continued to rise despite declining aircraft prices;
- few large orders would be placed – although the Saab 340 and the Saab 2000 together had about 34 per cent of the regional aircraft market;
- Saab had already cut costs internally.

After the presentation and lunch, separate meetings were held with each of the suppliers. During these discussions, Saab representatives showed how the price of the specific supplier's product had increased over the years. In this way, it was easy for the suppliers to see whether their product was among those that had risen in price, and how much compared against the total cost of purchased components. This aim of presenting the total situation in this way was to give a true picture of the situation.

During spring 1997 Saab Aircraft AB also visited some of the suppliers and discussed the situation with the management, and asked for a dramatic price cut. Each supplier was given information about the total cost of an aircraft divided between purchased components and in-house production as well as information about the supplier's part of the total cost of the purchased components. After this, as one of the Saab Aircraft managers noted, there were 'good arguments for lowering prices.'

Price reduction – but only 5 per cent

The 'cost-reduction campaign' ended in June 1997. The outcome was that some of the suppliers had lowered their prices as much as they had been asked to do, others lowered their prices less and still others did not lower their prices at all. Even though the 'cost-reduction campaign' was successful to some extent, the cost-reduction was not enough to lower the sales price of the aircraft. The price was still too high to be competitive.

The goal had been to lower the price of aircraft by 30 per cent. The percentage was based on information derived from the consultant company's database. After the campaign, the parties involved could see that it was impossible to reach the goal. Instead, the price reduction was about 5 per cent. This was because from the beginning, the supplier prices had already been at a lower level than those for other aircraft manufacturers.

On the basis of the earlier analysis and the outcome of the campaign, in summer 1997 Saab Aircraft AB came to the conclusion that it was impossible to continue production of the Saab 340 and the Saab 2000. It was time to begin planning an Ending Project.

Planning of the Ending Project

Planning of an Ending Project should start as soon as the project termination decision is taken. The planning process should follow the general recommendations concerning project planning. Like other projects, the Ending Project life-cycle has different phases (see Chapter 1), including the initiation, development, implementation, and termination phases. In an Ending Project, however, some of these tasks get more emphasis and, compared against projects that start from scratch, other solutions are already given. Essentially, it is important that stakeholders central to the project's network context are involved in planning the Ending Project.

All projects have some historic roots, such as prior references or long-term relations between the parties. This background has a special importance in an Ending Project: all of the earlier developments, interactions and goals linked with the main project affect how the Ending Project is seen and reacted to. It is not possible to start from a *tabula rasa*, an empty slate. Instead, it is a question of changing the *essential nature* of the project, which also makes the initiation of the Ending Project a demanding task. Therefore, both the general management level as well as the new project-ending organisation should be involved in the planning.

Involvement of the general management level in the initiation phase

It is important that the general management level is involved in the planning, and decides on

- the goal and the main guiding principles of the Ending Project
- the maximum cost limit
- the time limit, and
- the project-ending organisation.

Planning for such issues as costs and budgeting calls for less attention, as in a termination case they are more straightforward and given. In Box 3.3: The cost of termination we illustrate how the cost of ending the project was calculated in our example case. In the following box (Box 3.4: Deadline for the Ending Project) we show that the deadline, too, was more or less given in the example case, as the intention was for the termination to be completed when the last aircraft left the manufacturer's facilities.

Total estimated cost of termination: 4 billion Swedish crowns

The cost of terminating supplier relationships was an estimation based on the termination clauses in the agreements with the suppliers. Saab Aircraft AB had written agreements about twenty pages long with all of its 230 suppliers. These agreements included, amongst other things, terms governing after-sales support, including spare parts and technical maintenance. The agreement also had a clause stipulating how termination would be handled and the compensation the supplier would get in the case of termination. The Purchasing Department controlled each agreement, for example, with regard to the terms of the agreement should orders be cancelled.

The total cost of termination, including the settlement of obligations to personnel, was estimated at 4 billion Swedish crowns.

Box 3.4 Deadline for the Ending Project

One-and-a-half years of hard work

The Purchasing Department of Saab Aircraft AB, which originally had a staff of twenty-five persons, took care of renegotiating the contracts with suppliers. The time between the decision to terminate production and the cessation of production in spring 1999 was used to produce the last aircraft and to negotiate on contract termination or the conversion to a 'spare parts supply phase' with the roughly 230 suppliers.

While construction of the last aircraft and contract renegotiation were in progress, the whole production set-up, including the tools and jigs used for production, was being dismantled.

An important decision to be made by the general management is to define the type of ending project organisation and to appoint the project team. The Ending Project is usually best organised in one of two ways: the termination is carried out by the original project team or by a combined team made up of some original project team members and new team members. A third, but less desirable, alternative would be to appoint a totally new project team. This solution is less than optimal because important background information can easily be lost.

If the *original project team* is assigned the responsibility for the ending, the team members need a considerable reorientation in thinking. Their new tasks must be defined carefully, since they now must handle project termination. This may, for instance, involve difficult processes of crossing mental boundaries and overcoming feelings of failure. It is thus a very challenging situation for the project managers. On the other hand, the people who initially were responsible for the project have the best knowledge of the processes and developments so far, and thus they have a good basis for planning for the project termination. In addition, the original project team has taken part in previous interactions with the different parties and stakeholders, and thus knows them well.

When a new direction and radical changes are needed, as for instance in organisational reform, it is typical that new people are hired to execute these changes. A newcomer is free of historic ties and often brings a new and fresh interpretation of the situation at hand. Being free from earlier attachments, a newcomer often is more open to radical innovations. The challenge then is to motivate other involved parties for the changes. It is, therefore, often worthwhile to assign the termination task and strategy planning to an outsider, a *new responsible person*, who can work together with some members of the old project team to combine both old and new thinking and solutions. This was the situation in our example case.

In this book we concentrate on supplier relations, since the company's Purchasing Department became an important actor in the Ending Project. Three people at the Purchasing Department were appointed as the main responsible persons for the year-and-a-half it took to renegotiate all the contracts with the roughly 230 suppliers. For a discussion on how the case company organised the ending, see Box 3.5: The project-ending organisation. The company recruited a new managing director who took the key strategic decisions, and both managers and purchasers from the Purchasing Department shouldered individual responsibilities and were actively involved in the termination process.

Box 3.5 The project-ending organisation

Recruiting a new managing director

Before the final decision to terminate the production of regional aircraft was taken, Saab Aircraft AB hired a new managing director, Gert Schyborger, in 1997. His main responsibility was to analyse the situation at hand and thereafter to present a suggestion to Saab AB's Board of Directors regarding the future of the regional aircraft business. The new managing director had been involved in several mergers and thus had experience of working in a changing company. One of the managers at Saab Aircraft AB felt that the appointment of the new managing director came at a time '… when there was the feeling that now something was going to happen', and he continued that '… the step to take on a fellow who had experience of phasing-out [operations] was a clear sign.'

The Purchasing Department's enormous task

The management of the Purchasing Department consisted of three people, each of whom took the main responsibility for some of the suppliers. These three people had worked at the Purchasing Department more or less since Saab AB had once again started to produce commercial aircraft in the early 1980s. As one of the managers said: 'We had little turnover […] among the persons who took care of this.'

These three people handled all of the 230 suppliers. One of them noted that: 'We worked as a triad […] supporting the rest of the Purchasing Department.' However, the lion's share of the work was done by the purchasers. One purchaser was responsible for anything from two to three suppliers to as many as thirty to forty suppliers, depending on the complexity of the relationships. In some cases, the purchasers were so experienced that they could handle all of the negotiation work themselves as well as assisting other purchasers. Thus, each supplier had a main responsible person and a purchaser who took care of the renegotiations.

According to one of the main responsible persons, the difficulty was '… to run the whole process until a given aircraft number, to manage the suppliers so that we could obtain all the hardware we needed, and to manage our own personnel so that they would stay and assemble the last aircraft.' Responsibility for certain suppliers was delegated, but this did not always go smoothly as purchasers got new jobs, especially in cases where the new job was outside Saab AB and the purchaser left the company after the three-month notice period.

Who should be informed, and how?

After the decisions on goals, resources, deadlines and the project-ending organisation have been taken, the general management and the new project-ending organisation should together start to plan in greater detail how the termination will be executed. The following important questions, which are closely linked with the network context of the project, need to be answered:

- Who are the stakeholders?
- What is the message to the stakeholders?

A crucial point in planning of the Ending Project is to identify the different parties who need to be informed and/or involved. Anyone who has invested in the project, whether time, money, or both, is a project stakeholder. Thus, not only the project team is affected by the success or failure of a project; individuals and organisations in the project's network context, such as suppliers and customers, are also affected. When planning for the Ending Project, it is therefore important to consider all possible stakeholders.[7] Some of the stakeholders may be affected in a way different than expected, and their reactions may therefore be very different. In order to anticipate the long-term effects of project termination, it is important to approach the most important stakeholders first, while simultaneously also evaluating the impacts to and influences from the more extensive network of stakeholders.

In our example case, Saab Aircraft AB chose to involve and inform the most important suppliers, customers and the Swedish Government (see Box 3.6: Interacting with the most important stakeholders).

Box 3.6 Interacting with the most important stakeholders

Internal preparations before the official announcement

Before the final decision to terminate the production of regional aircraft was taken on 15 December 1997, Saab Aircraft AB notified the most important suppliers, customers, and the Swedish Government, and had negotiations with them. This occurred between October and December 1997.

After the decision was made to terminate aircraft production in August 1997, a period of two months was used for internal discussion as to how the message to external parties should be formulated. It was important to agree on the message, which was expressed by one of the managers at Saab Aircraft AB as follows: '... to be able to continue that kind of co-operation [...] it is very important to consider [...] how to express it already from the beginning [...] that the company has a united way of talking to the suppliers, so that there aren't any individuals who are allowed to do their own thing.'

The internal discussions concerned the overall strategy and the information to be given to the suppliers and to operators flying Saab aircraft. This was not seen as an easy task, as noted by one of Saab Aircraft AB's managers: '... it was very delicate [...] to find the overall strategy and the message that would then be channelled out to the supplier market and customer market. We were forced to rack our brains to find the best solution on this.' It was decided that the message to the suppliers would be as follows:

a)   The production of regional aircraft will be closed down.
b)   All ordered aircraft will be produced.
c)   Customers will be guaranteed future maintenance and access to spare parts.

Saab Aircraft AB strove to show all the suppliers involved that the situation was difficult and to give them as much time as possible to adapt to the new situation, since Saab Aircraft AB needed '... to keep the relationships intact because the products [...] will live an additional twenty years.'

During autumn 1997 the management of Saab Aircraft AB notified the management of the main suppliers directly. One of the supplier companies, for instance, felt that this was positive, as it meant that the supplier company would be able to inform its own employees before it became official. As one of the managers at the supplier company put it: 'Again, that is a great credit to them.'

No information was given to the press, because at the same time Saab Aircraft AB had negotiations with potential customers regarding sales of new aircraft. The reason for keeping the information within the management of Saab and its main suppliers at that stage was that, if it had become official that Saab Aircraft AB intended to stop producing regional aircraft, potential customers might have thought that the future of maintenance and spare parts would be unsure. This, in turn, might have influenced their purchase decision.

The official announcement on 15 December 1997

The Board of Directors of Saab AB decided to terminate the production of the Saab 340 and the Saab 2000 as from mid-1999. The fact that Saab actually did take this decision came as a surprise to many of the suppliers. Although the suppliers had seen that the number of orders had declined, and although Saab Aircraft AB had given notice that this might happen, the final decision still came as a surprise. One of the managers at Saab Aircraft AB noted that 'For many it came as a surprise that we in fact did make the decision, even though we had given notice several times that the situation looked grim.'

Immediately after the decision had been taken, customers were highly anxious about Saab Aircraft AB's ability to provide technical support and spare parts for the aircraft in the coming years. What would the future prices of aircraft maintenance be, for instance, once Saab was no longer producing the aircraft? One way of handling the anxiety was to send information directly to the operators. For example, the Saab Vice-President, Communications and Public Affairs, sent Crossair an e-mail on Wednesday, 17 December 1997.

For Saab it was important to maintain a good relationship with all of the suppliers who would supply spare parts in future. Considerable increases in spare part prices would make it dramatically more expensive for the operators of the Saab 340 and the Saab 2000. This, in turn, would mean that the operators would switch to other aircraft as soon as possible, leaving the Saab fleet on the ground. One of the managers at Saab Aircraft AB expressed this as follows: 'Our ambition was to try to keep the prices of spare parts at a low level so that we, in turn, would be able to offer normal prices to our operators.'

Once the stakeholders are identified, the planning of how to inform them begins. Different stakeholders call for different actions. As seen in our case and discussed further in Chapter 5, the connectedness of the stakeholders (in particular, their mutual exchange of information and interaction) complicates the challenges involved in handling the information and interaction.

Even though a project ends, this does not necessarily mean that the parties discontinue co-operating with each other. They may continue to work together on a new project. It is therefore important that the Ending Project is successful in the sense that bad feelings are kept to a minimum and the parties feel there is enough of a basis for future co-operation.

The timing of information sharing is crucial

The most important or critical stakeholders should be informed early on, before notifying stakeholders less affected by termination of the project. This early information sharing means, for instance, communicating with the project owner and the various stakeholders to give orders for change, to manage the changes and to motivate project team members.

Our example case has several areas where the right timing was critical for success. The timing of information sharing is one of these. Box 3.7: The critical time between the decision and the official announcement shows how the Ending Project might have fallen far short of success if open information sharing and interaction with the most important stakeholders had not been timed correctly.

Box 3.7 The critical time between the decision and the official announcement

The Swedish Government a big loser

Discussions with the Swedish Government, which had invested 1.5 billion Swedish crowns in risk capital, were held in autumn 1997 and took about two months. In September 1998, Saab AB owned 310 aircraft worth 11 billion Swedish crowns, a fact that did not make the situation any easier.

Time for the main customers to act before it would be too late

The Managing Director visited all the main customers in mid-October 1997 and told them frankly that the production of regional aircraft was threatened. As he said, 'We put all our cards on the table, we showed all the figures and everything.' He also informed the customers that this was the time to act if they wanted to have more Saab aircraft.

The customers were given three months to study their situation and to order as many aircraft as they needed before switching to another aircraft producer. It is not easy for operators to switch to another aircraft type, and so they needed time. The customers were satisfied with this procedure, as they '… could continue to live in peace and quiet with this fleet.' The outcome was thirty-five new orders during autumn 1997, which was seen as a good result. As the Managing Director notes: 'We received more orders when we had told [operators] that we were going to close than we had received when we tried to sell new aircraft.'

Saab Aircraft AB also got a substantial development order from Japan, ordering adaptation of the Saab 2000 model to be used for flight inspection. This development project continued throughout the whole termination period.

It was important to Saab that customers would continue to trust the company and its ability to maintain the existing aircraft, since many of them were leasing their aircraft. Had Saab not been able to convince them that the company would provide service, the operators would probably have returned the aircraft as soon as possible, which, in turn, would have meant additional loss. The severity of the situation was expressed by the Managing Director as follows: 'If we had not been able to convince customers that we would continue to take care of the aircraft so that they could continue to fly with them, we would have received them back. And in the worst case, that would have cost 11 billion.'

So the message Saab Aircraft AB gave its customers was: we will produce all the aircraft you order during the coming three months, and we will continue to take care of maintenance for the existing aircraft in the coming fifteen to twenty years. One of the managers at Saab Aircraft AB felt that the customers became calmer as they could see that '... Saab had a plan. We had activities in place to take care of this.'

Confidential information to the main suppliers

The management of the main suppliers was visited already in the beginning of September 1997, when they were told that the 'cost-reduction campaign' had not been successful enough. The suppliers were asked to stop production after a given aircraft number until they were given additional information, which they were promised would come in October–November.

In October, Saab Aircraft AB visited all the largest suppliers, some sixty to seventy companies accounting for about 80 per cent of the value of an aircraft. They were given more information about what would happen, and they were asked to start planning for the end of production. The suppliers were told that Saab's Board of Directors would take the final decision in December. Information was also given regarding the coming organisational changes concerning customer support, involving about 300 people. The important message was to convince the suppliers that Saab would continue to take care of the aircraft they had produced together.

The suppliers experienced the visits as positive because they were notified directly before the decision was official. As one of the managers at a supplier company said: 'Saab kept us informed of these matters and of its press release [...] considerably earlier. Its partners were informed before the matter was made public. We knew exactly what was going to take place. We knew about their decision process: we knew that their Board would be discussing the matter at such and such a time, and also that the Board would be making a decision on further action at such and such a time.'

The suppliers appreciated the company's activities, which provided them with a realistic picture of the situation. The same manager continues: '... For the entire duration of the project, Saab was exceptionally open to discussing the situation. [The discussion focused on] the likely situation for the next couple of years; its purpose was not to create an overly positive picture of the world but, in our opinion, to be rather realistic. As a result, we were [...] able to relatively well adapt our operations accordingly.'

Giving suppliers as much information as possible was also important from another point of view. Several of the suppliers had also been suppliers to the Fokker 50, the production of which had ended three to four years earlier. At that time the production company had gone bankrupt, which in turn meant that the suppliers got no compensation. According to one of the managers at Saab Aircraft AB: 'In the beginning, many were worried that our way of phasing out would be similar.' But owing to the backing of Saab AB, suppliers understood that bankruptcy would not come into question in this case.

Key features of the Ending Project

To summarise our discussion on planning for the Ending Project, as the boxes above have illustrated, it is the *planning* of the Ending Project that is important, not the *plan* in itself. About two-and-a-half years passed from the point in time when the company started to consider terminating the production of civil aircraft to the time when the Ending Project could be seen as finished. During this period, planning took place concerning, for instance, the goal and different sub-tasks, the project termination team and the information to be given, and the involvement of the stakeholders in the project network context. Changes were made in the planning, for example, when project team members left for new jobs or when stakeholders reacted in an unexpected way.

We propose that the termination of a project is a project in itself. Distinctive features of this type of project are:

* the reorientation of existing goals
* changes in commitment targets
* a radical change in the project nature (transformation), and
* often, a change in the people/team in charge.

While new projects are characterised by inspiration, vision and enthusiasm, an Ending Project focuses on bringing unfinished business to a proper end. Thus the skills required of managers and everyone else involved are very different in nature.

Moreover, there is a time-related issue when a project becomes an Ending Project. As seen in the example case, fundamental actions were taken to notify the pivotal parties at the appearance of the first negative signals. Before the final decision to terminate the project was taken, the company worked together with these parties in an effort to salvage production. This was one way of involving the central parties at an early stage. It was also a way of giving them extra time to adapt to the new situation. As the case illustrates, the stakeholders appreciated these efforts. Therefore, it is just as important to plan the timing of information as it is to plan for what the information will contain, who will give it and who will get it.

Key points for managers

* The general management level must be involved in the strategic decision-making on the ending of a project.
* The stakeholders should be identified and then notified and involved to the extent called for by their respective roles in the project.
* An Ending Project brings a history with it. Earlier developments, interactions and goals all affect how the latter phase – the Ending Project – is seen and reacted to.
* A successful Ending Project leaves the company image intact and does not hamper future business potential.
* The right timing of sharing information and involving stakeholders is crucial.

60   *V. Havila and A. Salmi*

Notes

1 Williams, Ackermann, Eden and Howick note that it is difficult to learn from complex projects, and in practice projects are often not reviewed at all. They concentrate on a case of project failure, and show that a professional focus on learning from the company's part helps the development of new processes. (Williams, T., Ackermann, F., Eden, C. and Howick, S. (2005) 'Learning from Project Failure', in Love, P., Fong, P. S. W. and Irani, Z. (eds) *Management of Knowledge in Project Environments*, Oxford: Elsevier, pp. 219–36.) In this book, we focus on the learning points from a successful Ending Project that is related to a complex initial project. As we see it, explicit focus on terminations will help companies to learn from their experiences and to increase their ending competences. These competences are in practice needed more often than the contemporary project management literature would indicate.

2 Davis, D. (2005) 'New Projects: Beware of False Economies', in *Harvard Business Review on Managing Projects*, Boston, Massachusetts: Harvard Business School Publishing Corporation, pp. 19–39. Originally published in *Harvard Business Review*, March–April 1985, p. 37.

3 Staw, B. M. and Ross, J. (2005) 'Knowing When to Pull the Plug', in *Harvard Business Review on Managing Projects*, Massachusetts: Harvard Business School Publishing Corporation, pp. 65–84. Originally published in *Harvard Business Review*, March–April 1987, pp. 65–75.

4 See, for instance, Turner, J. R. (1999) *The Handbook of Project-based Management*, 2nd edn, London: McGraw-Hill, p. 237.

5 Staw and Ross, op. cit., pp. 65–75.

6 Ibid.

7 Lake, C. (1998) *Mastering Project Management*, Thorogood.

4 Project-ending competence

In the previous chapter we discussed the Ending Project at the strategic level. We noted that planning the ending strategy calls for critical decisions by the general management. Here, we shall explore what happens during the execution of an Ending Project. In essence, this phase means that project-ending competences are harnessed, either by activating competences already existing within the company or, if competences are lacking, by acquiring them from outside the company.

The first two sections (Project-ending competence is rare, and What is project-ending competence?) discuss the characteristics of project-ending competence. The next section (How is project-ending competence gained?) examines how a company can attain the competence required, while its successor (Challenges for the Ending Project manager) presents the typical challenges managers encounter in executing the Ending Project. Finally, the key points are summarised.

Project-ending competence is rare

Termination of a project that does not follow the planned trajectory is always difficult. For example, the initial project members may have great difficulties accepting that the project is terminated. Also, various stakeholders may have negative feelings that influence the process and that potentially have negative consequences for the future. Therefore, project termination calls for special project-ending competence.

However, project-ending competence is very rare. Enthusiasm, action and experiences all tend to relate to the launching of new projects. Since projects by definition end sooner or later, at least during an on-going project, the ending phase is not considered to be complicated. Companies usually do not deliberately accumulate or develop any specific project-ending competence. Our example case illustrates very clearly that the situation at hand was not 'business as usual' for the individuals involved (see Box 4.1: A new task for the individuals involved).

Box 4.1 A new task for the individuals involved

The new situation facing the Purchasing Department

None of the twenty-five persons working at the Purchasing Department had earlier experience of terminating supplier contracts. As one of the managers put it: 'Emotionally you do not experience it as fun, but if you look at it from the professional angle it is very good to learn how to handle negotiations of this type, as they are often demanding and involve large amounts of money.'

New also for the suppliers

When the Purchasing Department and the suppliers went through the agreements, it became clear that the agreements did not cover a situation corresponding to that at hand, namely that termination was caused by 'the market'. The market was not buying the product, which meant that the minimum sales level was never reached. As expressed by one of the managers at a supplier company: 'It became obvious that, in fact, the agreement had no provision applicable to such a situation.' Thus, when the written agreements had been negotiated, none of the parties had experience of terminating production owing to external forces after only few aircraft had been produced, as was the case with the Saab 2000.

According to one of the suppliers, one reason for the lack of agreement terms applicable to a termination decision was that termination is an unexpected event; production lines usually more or less 'fizzle out', with a company seldom making a conscious decision to close a production line at a certain point in time.

As project termination is not a question of 'business as usual', it is often difficult to decide how much the Ending Project may cost. In our example case, estimation of the total costs of terminating the supplier contracts was based on the termination clauses in the earlier agreements. These in fact did not exactly cover the actual situation at hand. Thus the negotiators and decision-makers faced a rare, challenging – and, as it seems – also stimulating new situation that placed new demands on them.

The critical questions for managers in executing project termination are: What specific competences and skills are needed in the project-ending organisation, and how can these be gained and developed?

What is project-ending competence?

Project-ending competence means the ability and skills of the organisation and its employees to terminate the project so that internal and external project stakeholders and company relations incur as little harm as possible. The success of the Ending Project therefore depends partly on the organisation and partly on the ending-competences of specific individuals. In project termination, people count in many ways.[1]

Project-ending competence can be seen as an important aspect of a company's 'project competence'. Söderlund[2] sees project competence as an important strategic competence having four parts: project generation; project organising; project management; and team work. As we see it, one important element is missing: project ending. It is not enough for a company to be successful in project generation and execution; it is equally important to end projects that once were started.

As noted earlier, strategic, major decisions need to be made and empowerment of the ending team needs to be done at the upper echelons of the company, above individual project managers or project teams. Not only does the general management make the strategic termination decision, but they also need to *give fundamental support* to those carrying out the ending in practice. This is crucial in order for the operative level to be able to act (i.e., they need adequate resources and power) and willing to act (i.e., they must overcome their own commitment to the original project). In this way a solid basis for the Ending Project is formed.

The project-ending organisation must have *access to knowledge* concerning, for instance, how to terminate or renegotiate contracts, how to close operations, and how to deal with employees who need to be transferred elsewhere within the organisation or who will lose their jobs. This type of knowledge is often something that already exists within a company, but which now needs to be incorporated, in one way or another, into the Ending Project.

As discussed in Chapter 3, it is important to know who the stakeholders are. This means that one important part of an organisation's project-ending competence is *the knowledge and understanding of who the stakeholders are and what is important for them.* It is also critical to understand that the stakeholders' importance in an ending situation may differ from their importance when the project was started. The participants in the initial project have the experience and knowledge of the relationships with the different stakeholders and are thus also the best ones to anticipate potential problems that may occur during the Ending Project.

To be able to terminate a project successfully therefore may require many different types of expertise: management support; expertise in termination/

closing; and knowledge of the original project. If the company takes a strategic view of project termination, it also encourages development of the company's internal competences with regard to termination skills. These may then be put to use in other situations as well, thus improving the company's flexibility – a trait often needed in today's turbulent business world.

How is project-ending competence gained?

Project-ending competence can be gained in different ways. One way is to acquire competence from outside the company, by hiring or contracting experts. While helpful, this is inadequate for successful ending of a project. Success calls for a combination of both company-specific and project-specific knowledge in the termination process, and therefore the competence existing within the company is also needed.

Acquiring external competence

Often a separate 'exit champion' is needed, as Royer notes, to '... push [...] the organisation to admit when enough is enough.'[3] Moreover, an expert may have the skills required when ending a project – skills which differ from those required in the earlier phases of a project.[4] The 'exit champion' can be a person already working on the project or elsewhere in the company, but it is often wise to appoint a person free of earlier ties to this demanding role. To be successful, the 'exit champion' needs to have a high degree of personal credibility.[5] In our example case, Saab Aircraft AB decided to follow this route, namely to appoint a new Managing Director with experience of mergers and acquisitions, situations which often lead, for example, to the ending of relationships and even to closing down units (see Box 3.5: The project-ending organisation).

Another way of acquiring the necessary competence and know-how is to resort to different types of external consultants. These often play important roles both before and during the Ending Project.[6] In our example case, Saab Aircraft AB contacted a consultant company when they tried to avert the ending of production (see Box 3.2: Can we avoid ending?).

Furthermore, ending competence can be reached by reviewing other types of external advice. In our example case, Saab Aircraft AB also contacted a competitor who some years before had ceased aircraft production (Box 4.2: Contacting a competitor).

Box 4.2 Contacting a competitor

> At the end of February 1998 the three main responsible persons at the Purchasing Department of Saab Aircraft AB contacted a French competitor, ATR. ATR had previously ended production of turboprop aircraft for commercial use, and was thus expected to have experience of how to terminate supplier relationships of this kind. The visit to a competitor and the exchange of experiences was probably possible because British Aerospace was a part-owner of both ATR and Saab AB.
>
> This meeting in France did not yield much new input on how to deal with the suppliers, but more or less confirmed that the Purchasing Department's plans were correct. As one of the participants put it: 'I can't say that we heard any astonishing new things; instead we got support for the misgivings and problem areas that we had already identified. But it was also important to get confirmation of this.'
>
> The meeting in France confirmed the importance of ordering as many spare parts as possible for future use. In this way the company would be able to keep future prices for spare parts at a lower level, which, in turn, would be positive for future operators.

In this case, external advice was sought from a competitor company that had been in a similar situation earlier. This shows how closely linked different actors in a business field are, and how relevant information may also be obtained from sources that seem surprising at first view.

Mapping company-specific knowledge

Even though project-specific ending competence is rare, important knowledge that may be needed when ending a project can be found within the company. For example, communication with the Human Resource Department is important to find solutions concerning the future tasks and positions of employees who have been working on the project. Depending on the project type and length, there may be some individuals who have no natural home base to return to. A company's Human Resource Department also has knowledge concerning how to deal with retraining employees, retirement-related questions that may arise and personnel lay-offs. Therefore, when a project is being terminated, it is important to involve the Human Resource Department at an early stage.

Another reason to involve this department at an early stage is to demonstrate that project team members have no need to feel insecure. At least the people the company wishes to keep should be made well aware of this, otherwise there is a risk that performance will decline as the team members do not know what their next challenges will be.[7] Also, if key persons perceive a risk of unemployment, they may leave for new jobs before the project is wound up. This, in turn, may cause problems that are virtually impossible to solve, owing to the loss of project-specific knowledge.

One type of company-specific knowledge that requires careful consideration in the Ending Project is human resource management in a crisis situation. An Ending Project is always a crisis situation. It is a project no one would choose to be involved in and a situation that no one is interested in knowing about. For the general management, it is therefore important to allow the ending to be carried out within a specific project, the Ending Project, with its own identity. This is one way of recognising the importance of the original project and the work of team members, together with the termination efforts.

Our example case illustrates that, in the end, only a handful of the 1,800 employees who had worked on the Saab 340 and the Saab 2000 became unemployed, in part thanks to the efforts of Saab Aircraft AB (Box 4.3: How to deal with the 1,800 employees?)

Box 4.3 How to deal with the 1,800 employees?

In a press release of 24 September 1998, the Managing Director of Saab Aircraft AB said: 'The decision to cease producing regional aircraft was necessary for the company's future profitability and competitiveness. That does not make it less painful to be forced to give employees notice [...] although we now are doing our very best so that as few as possible will be unemployed ...'

Thus, Saab Aircraft AB needed to handle its relationship not only to external parties but also to 1,800 employees. The management's goal was that as many as possible would have a new job when aircraft production ceased.

Saab Aircraft AB worked actively to reduce the number of people who would have to leave the company. Besides those who got new jobs outside Saab, about 600 persons got new jobs within the Saab Group, roughly 100 persons were retrained, around 200 persons decided to accept the offer of early retirement, and some 400 persons continued to work for Saab Aircraft Customer Support and Saab Aircraft Leasing.

In September 1998, 475 persons were given notice, but in the end

Saab was forced to terminate the employment of only 111 workshop employees. This figure shrank further to fifty who did not have a job after production ceased in spring 1999.

Another company-specific ending competence that may be needed if contracts are terminated or renegotiated is the competence of solicitors. In our example case, Saab Aircraft AB chose not to involve the company solicitors directly in the negotiations, as shown in Box 4.4: When to involve solicitors?

Box 4.4 When to involve solicitors?

Most of the time, solicitors did not take part in direct negotiations with the suppliers, even though they were involved indirectly in some cases. The reason for this was, as one of the managers at Saab Aircraft AB said, that '... regarding the big ones we had contact with our solicitors, but tried not to take them with us to the negotiations. It is usually seen as an escalation if you come with a solicitor.' He continued that they '... did not want to invoke the clause on arbitration that is included in all contracts.'

Activating project-specific ending knowledge

In any Ending Project, the most important competence is the knowledge gained by the project team members during the on-going project. The individuals involved in the initial project have the best knowledge and understanding, for example, of the stakeholders. Involving team members from the initial project in planning and execution of its ending is one way to ensure that the different internal and external stakeholders' interests are looked after. However, as discussed earlier, these individuals often lack the knowledge of how to terminate a project in situations where this needs to be done in a way other than had been planned.

The important question is how to make each individual's knowledge explicit so that it can be used for the benefit of the Ending Project. In our example case, this was done by involving the whole Purchasing Department in planning both before the Ending Project started and during the Ending Project itself (Box 4.5: Involvement is the word). The weekly departmental meetings kept everyone involved informed about what was happening, and therefore they knew that the process was under control. The weekly meeting was also the place where both common and individual problems were solved.

Box 4.5 Involvement is the word

Brainstorming

The whole Purchasing Department retreated for a few days to plan how best to take care of the suppliers. It was decided to divide the suppliers into different categories:

* category A included suppliers strategically important for the future (to be able to ensure future maintenance and the supply of spare parts)
* category B included suppliers that were seen as important
* category C included suppliers for which there were alternative suppliers.

It was decided that category A suppliers would be visited in person. Many of these suppliers were large multinational companies, for which Saab was a small customer. There were about seventy suppliers of this kind. They were all visited and given information on such issues as why Saab was forced to terminate aircraft production, what the future looked like, how customer support would be reorganised, and what was expected of suppliers. As one of the managers at a supplier company stated: 'They came, they told us what was going to happen, they had written a letter to us which they asked us to sign. So it was, if you like, proof that we had indeed been told [...] and we had understood what they had told us [...] And I think we signed it and we [added] some words to it.' The same person continued: 'I think Saab actually handled it very well [...]. Giving bad news is hard [...]. Saab actually [...] did it in person, they told us and then went away and left us to digest it. I think that was quite valuable ...' The suppliers thus had the immediate possibility to ask questions. Saab Aircraft AB strove to make the suppliers accept that the previous agreement regarding the after-sales market would still be valid.

The other two supplier categories received a letter with the same information that had been delivered personally to the first supplier category. The suppliers were asked to sign the letter and return it, thus confirming that they had understood the situation and would not have any demands in the future. If they had any demands, the suppliers were asked to present them immediately.

Problem-solving at weekly meetings

To follow the negotiation process, the entire personnel of the Purchasing Department met weekly, and each purchaser reported what he/she had done during the week before, what he/she was going to do the coming week, and any problems that had surfaced.

The three supplier categories were used to monitor progress in negotiations – how much had been accomplished and how much of the negotiations with the suppliers still remained to be done.

The problems were discussed at the meeting, or afterwards one of the people mainly responsible assisted in solving the problem. One purpose of the weekly meetings was to spread experiences among the purchasers, as no one had prior experiences of this kind of work. One of the managers expressed it as follows: 'We also had meetings for the purpose of spreading experiences among us – how suppliers reacted, which arguments one should use – as no one could tell us how they had done it [before].'

Opportunity to learn new skills

The Purchasing Department personnel were encouraged to participate in the negotiations; this gave them the opportunity to learn new negotiation skills. As one of the managers at Saab Aircraft AB said '... there was so much to learn'. One of the persons interviewed expressed his feelings about the process as a whole by saying: 'I think that it was fun.' He saw it as a challenge and an opportunity to learn something totally new. However, he hoped that this would be the first and last time he was involved in closing down a large industrial project of this type.

A large and complex project typically needs a large project-ending organisation, often with separate projects. One project may deal with issues such as replacement of project team members, and another with purchasing and contracts with suppliers, to name a few possible sub-projects. In our example case, one sub-project was the Purchasing Department's project to renegotiate all the contracts with the roughly 230 suppliers (see Box 4.6: Sub-project purchasing).

Box 4.6 Sub-project purchasing

Spare parts: the crucial question for negotiations

One of the Purchasing Department's key goals in their negotiations with the suppliers was to ensure the building of new aircraft ordered by customers. Another goal was to negotiate agreements with suppliers that would guarantee the supply of spare parts, at costs as low as possible. One of the Purchasing Department managers stated: 'The goal for the sub-project was to ensure that we [...] would take home all [...] the material that was needed for production until the last aircraft we decided on [had been made].'

At the same time as the negotiations with suppliers were launched, the final orders for components were placed with suppliers. These orders included components for the new aircraft to be produced and spare parts that would be needed during the coming five to eight years. It was not an easy task to estimate this need; in the words of one of the managers: '... it was rather sensitive to determine exactly where we were, how many more shipsets we would need, and how many spare parts should be added on ...'

Challenges for the Ending Project manager

As seen here, project termination raises many types of managerial challenges. How these affect an individual manager depends on his/her position and role. There is a clear difference between general management and project management.[8] General management has legitimate authority and power of command, as laid down in a defined managerial hierarchy. The project management, in turn, has responsibility without rank or position, but it must have the ability to negotiate win–win results. These responsibilities and abilities are evaluated anew in the situation of project termination. Furthermore, the situation calls for the specific ending competences, especially from the Ending Project manager.

One important challenge for the Ending Project manager is to manage to keep the key project members until the project is ended, so that competent resources are ensured. A further challenge is to deal with the stressful situation successfully, so that the relationships with the various internal and external stakeholders continue to be good even after the project is ended.

Challenge 1: Keeping the key project members

One of the most important responsibilities for the Ending Project manager is to ensure sufficient human resources at all stages of termination. In our example case, this became an important issue, as the company received new orders at the same time as the Ending Project was started (see Box 4.7: Business as usual during the Ending Project).

Box 4.7 Business as usual during the Ending Project

It became highly important to keep as many of the employees as possible when new orders for thirty-five aircraft were received during autumn 1997. This meant that Saab Aircraft AB faced a new problem: How could the company retain the personnel for the next two years, so that all of aircraft orders could be filled, while at the same time the personnel were aware that Saab would cease producing regional aircraft? As one of Saab Aircraft AB's managers expressed it: 'Those who abandon ship first are the ones who are most attractive for the labour market, and often also the ones who are best suited for these jobs.'

Saab handled this by promising that none of the 1,800 employees would need to leave Saab without a new job. Starting in autumn 1997, each month the entire personnel received information about what had happened during the month and what would soon be happening. This information was given during half-hour meetings held in one of the hangars. The outcome was that during the last two years, all of the aircraft were produced on time and to a high quality. The Managing Director of Saab Aircraft AB expressed this as follows: 'Information is highly critical when you are going to change something.'

Therefore, special attention needs to be paid to the key human resources required in order to bring the project to its end successfully, as there is always the risk that pivotal individuals leave the project prematurely. These persons often have specific competences making it easy for them to find new positions. The best way to deal with this is to demonstrate early on that there will be new jobs waiting for the initial project team members after the project has ended.

Challenge 2: Managing a new type of team

If the members of the Ending Project team have participated in the project ever since the initial project was started, they are probably used to being in the centre of positive attention. The start of a project also means that the project team is expected to be creative and take initiatives, and there is usually a lot of enthusiasm.

In termination, the situation is totally different, as the upbeat spirit and optimism have been replaced by a sense of dullness.[9] No one is interested any longer in what the team is doing or, as one project manager once put it, 'no one wants any part of the funeral'. Furthermore, the Ending Project team members are usually not supposed to be creative or take initiatives, but instead to follow the limits set by the Ending Project. Thus, the Ending Project manager needs to be prepared to handle a team that is not always positive and enthusiastic about its work.

Often, the project ending also has wider effects on the organisation. In our example case (Box 4.8: From production to maintenance) the company, Saab AB, made a fundamental strategic change in ceasing the production of civil aircraft. This meant that the employees needed to change their way of thinking about the company and its identity. In situations when overwhelming changes are going to take place, bidirectional information – both giving and receiving information – is crucial.

Box 4.8 From production to maintenance

New identity

The aircraft will need spare parts and maintenance services for around twenty-five years into the future, i.e. during the period when the Saab 340 and the Saab 2000 are in traffic. This was expressed by one of the managers at Saab Aircraft AB as follows: '... it is the project that is closed, but the product continues to live on. So the business relationship is not terminated, but it passes into another phase.'

During the termination phase there was insecurity as to whether Saab Aircraft AB would be able to take care of the fleet and to develop and meet the demands of the authorities. One of the managers at Saab Aircraft AB said: 'The product is, in fact, no better than the actual customer support it gets. If we start to waver when it comes to supplying spare parts and technical customer support, training of engineers [...], then operators will not be able to keep [the aircraft] in the air any longer.'

One way to meet this insecurity was to form a customer support organisation that was made responsible for supplying the whole fleet with spare parts, training of technical personnel and updating of inspection, repair and maintenance manuals. About 100 engineers were transferred to the customer support organisation, as Saab also had to be able to continue developing the aircraft during its whole lifetime. As one of the managers put it: 'It was important to keep the engineer capacity [...]. And to invest in customer support.'

Thus, as from 1 August 1999, Saab Aircraft AB became a service company with around 320 employees in Linköping, Sweden, and about seventy employees in Washington, USA, who sell spare parts and maintenance services to operators using the fleet comprising 459 Saab 340 and sixty-three Saab 2000 aircraft.

New contact persons

The organisational change also meant that there would be new people at Saab Aircraft AB to take care of the supplier relationships. For suppliers, too, it was probable that there would be new people, as different organisational units usually handle development, production and after-sales markets. As concluded by one of the managers at Saab Aircraft AB: 'In other words, it is new organisations that will work together.'

As soon as one year after the new contract between Saab Aircraft AB and the Finnish company Patria Finavicomp Oy was signed, the responsible persons in Finland no longer knew whom to contact at Saab Aircraft AB. They knew that many of their previous contact persons still worked at Saab AB, but they did not know what these people's tasks were at the moment. This became obvious to one of the managers in Finland when he got a telephone call from a person in their Maintenance Department asking whom to contact at Saab AB: 'It made me think, but I didn't really know [...]. I said that the number of the switchboard was such and such and that they could try to ask there. I wasn't able to give any other advice.'

Some individuals may have difficulties in accepting project ending, even more so when the project is terminated in an unexpected or abrupt way. Whether consciously or unconsciously, they may even spread ill-will if they are not informed about the developments appropriately and frequently.

Therefore, the key for successful management of relations with the initial team members is efficient communication and information sharing.

Challenge 3: Managing all of the relations at the same time

Often a project is part of a programme made up of several different projects. It is thus necessary not only to manage individual projects but also to co-ordinate several projects simultaneously. The tool for co-ordinating projects having a shared business aim is programme management, which becomes even more critical when one of the projects within the programme is terminated. A project manager often does not have enough knowledge of the project owner's other projects that may be affected when one project is terminated. For example, it is important that a project owner's relationships to the stakeholders of its other projects are not disturbed when one of the projects is terminated.

One way to respond to this challenge is to ensure that each individual knows his/her responsibilities within the Ending Project. It should be clear, for example, who is expected to deal with the various stakeholders and what message should be given to them. This helps avoid harmful developments in relationships during the Ending Project and helps keep the stakeholders satisfied. This is also a way to avert false rumours and to keep 'waves of uncertainty' from starting to spread among the stakeholders.

Next, in Chapter 5, the issue of connections in the context of the Ending Project is discussed further.

Key points for managers

* Ending competence means the ability and skills of both the organisation and its employees to terminate the project so that as little harm as possible is done to the internal and external project stakeholders and company relations.
* Ending competence is to a large extent made up of the visions and skills of the people involved.
* The success of the Ending Project depends partly on the organisation and partly on the ending competences of specific individuals.
* Ending competence as such exists in companies only rarely, but may be developed and gained to some extent.
* Knowledge of how to end a project can be acquired from the original project, from elsewhere in the company and from outside the company.
* The key challenges in execution of the ending are how to retain the key persons and how to deal with a situation that is difficult and stressful to all parties.
* If it is handled well, an Ending Project increases the company's internal

competences with regard to termination skills; these may be utilised in other situations, thus improving the company's flexibility.

Notes

1 Spirer, H. F. and Hamburger, D. H. (1988) 'Phasing Out the Project', in Cleland, D. I. and King, W. R. (eds) *Project Management Handbook*, 2nd edn, New York: Van Nostrand Reinhold, p. 235.
2 Söderlund, J. (2005) *Projektledning & projektkompetens. Perspektiv på konkurrenskraft*, Malmö: Liber AB.
3 Royer, I. (2005) 'Why Bad Projects Are So Hard to Kill', in *Harvard Business Review on Managing Projects*, Boston, Massachusetts: Harvard Business School Publishing Corporation, pp. 85–108. Originally published in *Harvard Business Review*, February 2003, p. 86.
4 Turner, J. R. (1999) *The Handbook of Project-based Management*, 2nd edn, London: McGraw-Hill, p. 330.
5 Royer, op. cit., p. 103.
6 Staw, B. M. and Ross, J. (2005) 'Knowing When to Pull the Plug', in *Harvard Business Review on Managing Projects*, Massachusetts: Harvard Business School Publishing Corporation, pp. 65–84. Originally published in *Harvard Business Review*, March–April 1987, p. 81.
7 Turner, op. cit., p. 333.
8 Mantel, S. J. Jr et al. (2001) *Project Management in Practice*, New York: John Wiley & Sons, p. 3.
9 Spirer and Hamburger, op. cit., p. 231.

5 Managing the network context of an Ending Project

When starting an Ending Project, it is extremely important not only to identify the stakeholders but also to understand how to deal with them. Stakeholders that are directly and continuously connected with the project, such as the project owner, project manager and project team, are relatively easy to handle during the Ending Project, as in principle their role is clear. Indeed, their relevance to the project will gradually decrease in importance and they will eventually disappear when the project is wound up.

In this chapter we concentrate on stakeholders whose role *vis-à-vis* the Ending Project is more *complex*. To give an example, if a supplier relationship continues after project termination, as for instance when the supplier is a supplier for other projects of the company, co-operation between the parties continues on a different basis. This means that even though the project is terminated, the relationship between the parties will still continue. For another supplier relationship, in turn, termination may be the only feasible solution once the project has ended. Then it is crucial to handle this termination process successfully, in order to ensure future business potential.

Another key concern here is the different *connections* relating to projects. In particular, we investigate how these connections affect, or are affected by, project termination. The relevant question for managers to address is how to cope with the complexities of the stakeholder relations and connections in the network context.

We start (The first step: identifying different connection types) by identifying the different types of connections that are present in the network context of the Ending Project. We discuss how the projects are connected to other projects, how the stakeholders are connected amongst themselves, how changes may spread within the network context, and how the issues of timing and dynamics affect the termination processes. Then (The second step: managing complexity) we present ways of dealing with the complexities: how to handle groups of stakeholders and influential stakeholders, and how to cope with differing perspectives *vis-à-vis* the network context of the project. In the following section (Success in project termination) we conclude our discussion on the empirical case by investigating the success of this Ending Project. Finally, the key points for managers are summarised.

The first step: identifying different connection types

In Chapter 2 we indicated the importance of recognising the network context of the project. By the 'network context' we mean the different actors connected with the project either directly or indirectly, through the actors who are connected directly. In project termination, it is extremely important to delve further and to focus on the various connections between the stakeholders. Sometimes even peripheral actors in the project's network context may have an impact on the developments and results of termination. Therefore, we see identification of the connections involved as the first managerial step in managing the network context.

Projects are connected

An important connection to consider is the connection between different projects. Traditional project management literature considers connections in terms of how projects are linked, that is, the role of various projects within a programme or portfolio of projects. Co-ordination of projects is often seen as having clear steps that are related to the different links between the projects.[1]

As our discussion so far has shown, the co-ordination tasks involved in terminating complex interorganisational projects are demanding. They cannot be solved with simple practical tools; strategic thinking is also necessary. This is because not only the projects but also their respective stakeholders may be connected. This overlap of connections means that when one project is terminated, the company needs to consider carefully the effects on the network contexts of other projects.

To illustrate this point, we can examine the situation of the Finnish supplier in our empirical case. This supplier was involved in both projects: development of the successful Saab 340, and development of the Saab 2000. As the supplier base for the two aircraft types differs to some extent, involvement in the second project meant new contacts for the Finnish supplier and the potential for internationalisation. (See Box 5.1: Positive connections between the two development projects.)

Box 5.1 Positive connections between the two development projects

Patria Finavicomp Oy (part of the Finnish aerospace and defence group, Patria) develops and manufactures structures ranging from commercial aircraft to space satellites. It became a supplier of machined parts for the Saab 340 in 1983–84. The company became involved in the Saab 2000 project in 1989, and produced the tail for the aircraft.

Through this new co-operation, Patria Finavicomp Oy became more international, which was one of the goals when the co-operation started. Another goal was to increase company know-how of advanced composites. As one of the managers said: '... we would not have participated in the project if it had not brought some new technology to the company [...]. We went along because the project had two targets. Firstly, the development of new technology: composite and bonding technology. The second target was to establish a longer-term business relationship, which would take us to the international market. Of course, there was a third target: a successful project [...]. We have those investments [...]. We acquired know-how and went global. What did not happen was that it never produced the expected financial results.'

For this supplier the two projects initially were positively connected, as they enabled the company to develop its technological basis. For Saab Aircraft AB, the connection between the two development projects was also positive. However, this connection became a problem when market conditions associated with the Saab 2000 forced the company to terminate production of its successful aircraft, the Saab 340, as well.

When termination occurs, the connections between projects may easily become liabilities. It is therefore especially important to consider the overlapping network contexts of the company projects.

Stakeholders communicate with one another

Very different kinds of stakeholders (for instance, suppliers, customers, state organisations, local residents, non-government organisations or banks) may have a stake in the project without being connected amongst themselves. They do not necessarily interact with one another; they may not even be aware of each other. However, as discussed in Chapter 2, several stakeholders are connected, some even very tightly. If this is the case, when terminating a project it becomes critical to consider these connections.

The earlier literature on business networks convincingly demonstrates how individual business relationships are, in fact, interconnected in many ways. Therefore, changes taking place in any one of them rapidly spread to the larger networks of relationships.[2] Thus, management of change – and particularly termination of projects – calls for sensitivity to the connectedness of relations.

In our example case, it was clear that the company immediately had to consider a large number of (interconnected) relations. Our earlier discussion of the company's strategic planning and activities shows how the company approached several stakeholder groups and managed individual relations simultaneously. The effects of the termination process were spreading quickly, with one reason being that the suppliers immediately began communicating amongst themselves, as described in Box 5.2: Suppliers communicate directly with one another. This communication also gave suppliers a common basis for actions.

Evidently, there is a real need to address the visible and potential connections between the stakeholders. Indeed, it is crucial that stakeholders are not given contradictory information. However, consistency does not mean that everyone must receive exactly the same information. In some cases, for instance, the parties may have agreed to share more information – and such disclosure agreements naturally must be followed.

Box 5.2 Suppliers communicate directly with one another

During the renegotiations it became obvious that some of the suppliers had contacted each other, as expressed by one of the managers at Saab Aircraft AB: 'It is so obvious when they have spoken with each other. There are claims that are similar.' This made the negotiators from Saab Aircraft AB realise that whatever they did in one relationship might influence another relationship. It was therefore important to be consistent in all the negotiations.

For a supplier, communication with other suppliers was one way of attempting to cope with the difficult situation. For example, the two companies producing the wing and the tail contacted one another every time they had received 'news' from Saab. A representative of the tail-producing supplier stated: 'We were in frequent communication with Casa [...] whose leader for this project was [...]. We talked with him rather often, specifically about the way Saab was behaving and the information it was providing and, in a way, we were cross-checking whether we received the same kind of information [...] we also

> discussed the possible cost-related consequences of the termination procedure [...] and what the agreement provided for [them] and what it provided for us [...]. In this way, we tried to ensure that if one of us obtained something under a clause, the other could invoke the same clause.'

There are connections over time

History and developments over time matter in business relationships and networks – in many different ways. In our example case, the renegotiations with suppliers showed that counterparts' reactions were affected by the stakeholders' view of past developments. Moreover, not only what has happened in the actual relationship between the parties is important; also important is what has happened in the supplier's relationship with other customers (as seen earlier in Box 2.2: History matters). All relationships with the stakeholders in the network context of a project are thus charged with earlier experiences, and these affect how termination of the project is seen and the reactions to it.

In addition, relationships and stakeholder views are affected by the parties' expectations for future business. If there is a high chance of new projects or other co-operation, all parties are more keen on conducting the termination under conditions that are as positive as possible. Once termination is completed, the era comes for new potential and the start of new business. After the Ending Project, the company should ensure a smooth transition to 'business as usual'.

In general terms, we may investigate the time dimension by exploring the linkages between the different periods of project termination: firstly, we find the initial project, followed by the Ending Project and finally the era of new business. Activities during all these periods affect what the end result of termination will in fact look like. For instance, after the Ending Project, the ending organisation will be dissolved and people will move on to other tasks. After a relatively long and intensive co-operation phase, this organisational closure may be one issue causing problems in the stakeholder relations.

In our empirical case, these linkages are clearly visible. Firstly, the termination process was affected by the initial product development and production, and this, secondly, laid the basis for the future. The ending team only handled the renegotiations, and new people with different skills and competences (the Customer Support Department) stepped in later to handle aircraft maintenance and support operations. In this case, the temporal project organisation vanished overnight. The earlier partners experienced this to some extent negatively, as exemplified earlier by the Finnish supplier's comment on how difficult it was to find a contact point once the project organisation had been dismantled (see Box 4.8).

Furthermore, in Chapter 3 we investigated in detail the issue of the timing of information sharing – it is critical to approach key stakeholders early on, but also to consider the spreading of information amongst them. Thus, the right timing of information becomes important, not least because the network effects of termination start immediately.

To conclude, different dynamic and time-related processes take place in project termination. Some of these call for careful strategic planning while others are more tactical by nature – requiring, for example, communication skills in practice. Either way, the developments over time need to be considered, rather than focusing only on the present (tactical) problems. While the time window for termination actions may be short, these actions have long-term effects.

Changes spread far via indirectly connected relations

The starting point for all network analysis is to realise the intangible features of networks and the impossibility for any single actor of controlling them.[3] While the company may try to influence its direct business partners and to mobilise them for joint action, it is impossible to control even direct relations – in the end, the actions of two parties are needed for all interaction.

Therefore, indirect connections in the network context become even more difficult issues to handle. Also in the Ending Project, these cannot be controlled. Still, as noted in Chapter 2 and illustrated in Figure 2.1, even indirectly connected actors belong to the network context of the Ending Projects. Therefore, the company needs to be prepared for actions that take place in the indirect relations: for instance, sub-suppliers and end-customers become easily affected by the termination, such as when rumours spread among the connected actors, affecting the company image.

Our empirical case also has examples of indirect connections. To start with, one initial reason that set into motion the entire ending process was the reactions of end-customers – passengers who considered turbo-propeller aircraft to be old-fashioned. Later on, actors in the supply chain were affected by the termination of production of the Saab 340 and the Saab 2000 (see Box 5.3: Changes are spread in different ways). This illustration discusses the sub-suppliers (suppliers to the direct suppliers). In most cases, the termination had little impact on the relationships between the sub-suppliers and the main suppliers. In some cases, however, the relationships with the sub-suppliers were terminated as well. Therefore, termination of the project brought both incremental and radical changes[4] in the direct and indirect relations of the central company, Saab Aircraft AB.

Box 5.3 Changes are spread in different ways

For one supplier, about ten sub-suppliers were affected by the termination of production. The supplier applied different strategies *vis-à-vis* its relationships, and also communicated in different ways with the sub-suppliers. Relationships with one or two minor sub-suppliers were completely terminated following the termination of production. Two or three companies received more information that the work would be coming to an end. This was because the company needed to calculate the quantity of raw materials and ready-made components that the sub-suppliers had in their warehouses relating to the Saab 340 and the Saab 2000. Finally, some suppliers were advised in passing about the situation. These were suppliers that supplied goods worth only a small amount of money or that would get other orders from the company instead. This meant that the business remained more or less at the same level.

The situation regarding the Finnish company, Patria Finavicomp Oy, was different. It had few sub-suppliers for the products it sold to Saab Aircraft AB, and therefore Saab Aircraft AB's production termination had little additional impact on the Finnish side. Also the fact that termination took place over a long time period kept the consequences for the sub-suppliers relatively small. This was expressed as follows by one of the managers at Patria Finavicomp Oy: 'It came to an end over such a long time span. It was not the kind of stoppage that would have upset anyone's life very badly.'

To conclude, each project has it own unique network context (see Chapter 2), and it is important that this network be considered when planning for the termination of a project. In this chapter we have deepened the discussion of the reasons underlying the uniqueness of each project network context, thus pointing to the prevailing connections. Next it is critical to analyse how to cope with the complexity arising from these connections.

The second step: managing complexity

We have highlighted the many connections figuring in developments in the network context of an Ending Project. It is clear that there are many challenges, and one may wonder whether it is possible to cope with all the complexities. We propose that the solution is to consider the strategies for different stakeholder groups and for influential stakeholders, and also to try to understand how others see the network context of the project.

Dealing with different stakeholder groups

The stakeholders of a project can be grouped into categories on different dimensions. One typical way is to analyse stakeholders' role in the project (e.g., customers, suppliers, financers, local citizens). These categories are important, since different stakeholder groups have different needs in project termination. Furthermore, the company can form different strategies for each stakeholder group, or even for their sub-groups. For example, suppliers may need information differing from that needed by customers or project sponsors. In addition, different sub-groups of suppliers may require different strategies. Moreover, it is very important to realise that the different stakeholder groups are also connected – for instance, what happens to customers in project termination also affects the project suppliers.

Secondly, stakeholders can be categorised according to the degree to which they will either affect or be affected by the project and project termination. This analysis helps to identify the stakeholders having critical roles in the termination phase. This is important, as these stakeholders may not have been central for the network context of the initial project but take on a key role in termination. We shall explore the topic of the most influential stakeholders in the next section.

Grouping of stakeholders is efficient and often necessary, as it enables handling a large number of network actors. Saab Aircraft AB's way of executing one part of the Ending Project (concerning supplier relations) is a good example of this. The approach they followed shows how it was possible to deal simultaneously with more than 230 external stakeholders with only around twenty-five persons in charge.

The key stakeholder groups in this Ending Project were easy to identify: first and foremost, the *suppliers* were critical. The case shows that suppliers can be an important stakeholder group in both the short run and the long run. The suppliers were needed for deliveries during the Ending Project, but many of them were also needed afterwards. The second key group is *customers*. Saab Aircraft AB acted very attentively towards this group in the first phases of the Ending Project, even before making the final decision to end production, as seen in Chapter 3. As far as the third stakeholder group, *public organisations*, is concerned, the Swedish Government was important. As the state had invested in development of the aircraft, there was a reason to 'keep the aircraft flying'. The fourth stakeholder group is internal to the company: the *general management* was involved, as terminating production of the two aircraft types had to be managed along with SAAB AB's other operations and production programmes.

The two stakeholder groups that became extremely important in the Ending Project are discussed further in Box 5.4: Two important stakeholder groups. Firstly, the company had to ensure the supplies of spare parts and maintenance, which placed suppliers into a special category among the stakeholders. It was critical to assess the relationships with suppliers and to renegotiate contracts with them. Furthermore, for strategic actions, the company grouped its suppliers into three categories, as was shown earlier in Box 4.5. Secondly, the customers, i.e. the operators flying the Saab 340 and the Saab 2000, were important. They had to be convinced that the aircraft would be in perfect shape for the next twenty to twenty-five years. As seen earlier, the company succeeded so well that it even made new contracts despite termination.

Box 5.4 Two important stakeholder groups

Even though production was going to cease, this was not the case with most of the supplier relationships, as the existing aircraft would need to have maintenance and spare parts for the next twenty to twenty-five years. Therefore, Saab Aircraft AB started the process of negotiation with all of the suppliers. One of the managers at Saab Aircraft AB notes: 'We could not just go to our suppliers and say that we are going to break this off now. Instead, we were forced to negotiate with them, to pay them if that's what they wanted, and to get them to accept that they would continue to deliver parts in lesser quantities.'

Especially with regard to the Saab 2000, Saab Aircraft AB was aware of that the reaction from the suppliers involved would not be positive or easy to handle. This was expressed as follows by one of the managers: 'In some way we had to retain a relationship with them so that we [could] continue to work together. And that [was] not so easy, because some of [the suppliers] who got involved in the 2000, for example, [...] invested money and thought that it would be a few hundred aircraft so that they would get back the money [they had invested].'

Suppliers that had been involved in developing the Saab 340 aircraft had been able to recoup their development costs. Therefore, the negotiations with them were not expected to be difficult. One of the managers stated: 'They think that they have been able to deliver a certain amount already [...] so they shrug their shoulders and say that it must end one day anyhow.'

It was extremely important to continue most of the relationships with the suppliers, and also to convince the operators. The company had to show that it would be able to guarantee the future supply of spare parts so that the operators would continue to fly the Saab 340 and the Saab 2000. The same manager at Saab Aircraft AB continued: 'We could not destroy the relationships; instead we had to make the customers believe that even though we were going to close down [...] Saab would be there and that we would [...] ensure that this would work.'

The example nicely illustrates how two different types of stakeholder groups are connected with one another during the Ending Project. For the management, this means that the stakeholder groups should not be handled separately; instead, the ending strategy should consider the possible connections between the groups.

For example, Supplier X's power to influence a project may be appreciably stronger than Supplier Y's power. On the other hand, the company may have customers with a differing influence: powerful Customer A and less powerful Customer B. For the ending strategy this may mean that influential Supplier X and the important Customer A should be handled in a similar way. Thus, the reference point is not only the stakeholder group, but also the power position of an individual stakeholder, and further, their connections.

Indeed, stakeholder grouping is only one – and in our view an insufficient – basis when planning for the ending processes. Different connections and relations play a role, too.

Dealing with influential stakeholders

Depending on stakeholders' power of influence and the extent to which project termination may affect them, some stakeholders can be seen as the primary stakeholders.[5] Moreover, a stakeholder's power of influence during an on-going project may differ considerably from that during the termination phase. Therefore, the stakeholder groups do not provide a tool powerful enough for management – we need to look at the specific features of stakeholders.

The industrial network approach to connections between companies provides one method for investigating individual stakeholders' power of influence.[6] According to this approach, business relationships can be analysed by using the following three 'layers': *resource ties*, *activity links*, and *actor bonds*.

Resource ties describe how the companies' resources are tied together. For example, a supplier company's production equipment used to make the wings for aircraft must be adapted to meet the customer's specifications for the final products. Activity links, on the other hand, describe the activities of the two companies linked together by the relationship. This might be, for example, how the production of wings at the supplier company is linked with production of the final aircraft at Saab Aircraft AB. Finally, actor bonds describe the relationship between the interacting actors (individuals, organisations, units), which can be characterised, for instance, by the type of commitment and trust existing between the two parties. Actor bonds are to a large extent based on the perceptions of the interacting individuals.

Thus, the supplier of the wings can only sell the product to Saab Aircraft AB, as the wing construction is aircraft-specific. Conversely, Saab Aircraft AB can only buy the wings from the specific supplier. These resource and activity connections mean that the two parties are tied to a long-term business relationship. This departing point easily leads to mutual commitment, which, in turn, would also affect project termination.

In the example case (see Box 5.5: Changes in supplier power), it became apparent that suppliers not critical in the initial project may become important during the ending phase. This indicates how different stakeholders, although belonging to the same group (that of suppliers), had to be approached differently, depending on their power of influence during the Ending Project.

Box 5.5 Changes in supplier power

Production systems are tied together

Some of the 230 suppliers to the two Saab aircraft turned out products that took up to eighteen or even twenty-four months to produce. This means that when Saab AB 'pushed the stop button' in December 1997, these suppliers had already produced some components and purchased some raw materials that would never be used for their intended purpose. Some of these could be put to other uses, while others were specially designed for the Saab aircraft and were thus useless. It was clear that these suppliers would demand compensation. However, this was seen as a relatively easy aspect of the negotiations since, as one of the managers stated: '... it is rather tangible and objective, either they exist or they don't [...]. One only needs to pay and look happy after one has checked that the price is right.'

Typical areas in the negotiations concerned compensation for production tools and drawings, as well as compensation for a lesser production pace.

Suppliers who made products needed at the beginning of the aircraft production line ended production more or less immediately, whereas those who were involved in later phases of production continued with their own operations. The last part for the last Saab 2000 was delivered to Saab in Linköping in November 1998. For some of the suppliers, the interval between having been informed of the final termination decision and cessation of production for Saab was thus about a year.

Impact of earlier activities

The most demanding negotiations involved suppliers that had invested money in product development. Most of them were suppliers of structural parts. This was expressed by one of the managers at Saab Aircraft AB as follows: 'The most difficult ones to settle were the ones that had large production facilities of their own, for which they had invested their own capital. They were mainly those [suppliers] who produced parts for the fuselage.'

In some of the supplier relationships, Saab Aircraft AB was forced to accept less advantageous terms in order to secure the supply of spare parts: 'It has cost money in some cases'. For example, in one of these cases, the supplier had been forced to make major modifications to its product several times. This supplier had invested enormous sums of money in development and improvement of the product, sums which were sunk costs in the new situation.

Commitment is important

Prior developments affect the parties' commitment to the relationship and to one another. This commitment becomes critical in ending. One of the supplier relationships had a special history: some five years earlier, Saab Aircraft AB had terminated the relationship and started to buy from another supplier. It later emerged that Saab Aircraft AB was unable to find a supplier for all the parts this original supplier had supplied, and therefore Saab had to begin the business relationship anew. In the termination situation, this supplier took advantage of the opportunity and raised the prices of spare parts considerably. One of the managers at Saab Aircraft AB noted that: 'five years later they hadn't forgotten what we did'. Mutual trust and commitment had been lost in the past, and in termination this provoked a negative reaction from the supplier.

Understanding others' view of the network context of the project

The connections discussed here make our approach different from that in many project management texts. Stakeholders are discussed often, of course, but they are usually taken as a group of individuals or organisations that do not form relationships or interact amongst themselves.[7] Thus their connections are not considered.

Within project marketing, Cova and Salle[8] stress the relationships between the stakeholders of a project rather than the actors themselves. They discuss the collective body of the key actors, which they term the 'milieu'. Importantly, they also note that the milieu has a set of rules and norms that regulate interaction. According to Cova and Salle, these developments in project marketing would also benefit project management thinking, and we agree.

Indeed, the common norms for behaviour, built up during the initial project within the network context, play an important role when the project is terminated. In the case of a long-term project, the initial project may form many rules that everyone follows. In termination, these behavioural norms (the history) affect how the final phase unfolds. This also explains why stakeholders may remain very committed to one another even in termination. Alternatively, if earlier norms have encouraged opportunistic behaviour, termination may quickly become a crisis situation for many. All these aspects indicate how the interactive dimension – i.e., the relations between the network members – plays a role in project terminations.

Relationships are not tangible, and their analysis is based on the perceptions of each individual involved in them. Thus, the view of the network context of an ending project and the individual's perspective on it depend on the position of the individual and the company in the network. For instance, there are differences in 'network horizons' that illustrate how widely the individual can perceive different connections beyond the most direct ones. These horizons have also been used to analyse, for example, how changes spread in business networks.[9]

As perceptions matter, there is no objective, tangible network context to be fully understood by anyone. Each person interprets the situation in a different way. Ford, Gadde, Håkansson and Snehota[10] propose that these differences may be captured by 'network pictures'. Each network actor has its own unique 'picture' of the network, which is comprised of the actor's perceptions of what is happening in the network. This, in turn, is based on previous experiences. The network therefore looks different from different angles, and the picture of the network depends on the point of observation. The network pictures can be used to form a basis for the strategies to be applied in managing relations with different stakeholders during the Ending Project. In this way, one can gain a better understanding of the network context relevant for the Ending Project.

Therefore, when terminating a project, managers need to understand the network context of the project not only from their own perspective, but also from the perspective of others. Thus, to some extent they should try to put themselves into the shoes of important stakeholders and then picture how the network context looks. This helps the management to anticipate probable reactions to the termination and may make it easier to handle the connectedness of relations.

Network pictures are unique, but to some extent they are overlapping. The more similar they are, the easier it is for the parties to understand each other's behaviour. An example that illustrates a situation of overlapping network pictures is the view of the common 'enemy' shared by Saab Aircraft AB and the Finnish company, Patria Finavicomp Oy. Both companies agreed that the common enemy – the reason for termination – was 'the market'. This, in turn, had a positive impact on the atmosphere of the Ending Project (see Box 5.6: A common view on the reasons for ending).

Box 5.6 A common view on the reasons for ending

Early understanding of the negative signs

Patria Finavicomp Oy was well aware of the signs indicating that the Saab 2000 project might not be successful, and had started to prepare for the worst. This was expressed as follows by one of the managers: 'The production never reached the anticipated volume. Quite early, the feeling was that it would fail. In consequence, the termination was not catastrophic to operations.'

Sharing the risk

Patria Finavicomp Oy was one of the risk-sharing partners, and had accepted this in the original agreement. There was no question of exercising any of the termination clauses in the agreement, as the agreement had no provisions for a situation corresponding to the one at hand. As one of the managers noted: 'Since this agreement with Saab was terminated in this way [...] the market tumbled. It is part of the risk that a risk-sharing partner takes. If it had terminated in some other way, there would have been clauses applicable to it. [...] In other words, everything was ready for such a case, but not for a situation like this.'

Common understanding during negotiations

One reason why the negotiations between these two parties were not perceived as difficult was the common understanding of the fact that it was 'the market' that caused the termination. The Finnish side stated: 'The end of the project caused no grudge-bearing rift between Saab and us. It was not a question of the business relationship but rather the tumbling of an external market.' The Swedes had a similar view: 'In Finland, they said: "OK, such things happen, so what, it has to be accepted. What shall we do with the spare parts?" And then we reached an agreement on that.'

However, one problem was the small number of aircraft produced, which made the situation difficult for all parties. One of the managers at Saab Aircraft AB pointed out that '... there was a clause in the contract that said that there will be no compensation if we have to close down because there is no market. That is their market risk [...] When we stopped [production] as early as after about sixty units, it was a very bitter pill to swallow.'

Negotiations proceeded smoothly despite the difficult situation. One likely reason was that the parties understood each other and each other's way of doing business. This was mentioned by one of the Finnish managers: 'For us and Saab, it is easy to lay the foundation for this kind of business relationship since our cultures, our way of thinking, are so similar [...]. It was as if the same logic was used to construct the level of thought [...]. When some Kjell or Lennart said on the phone that you'll get such and such an amount for something if you proceed in a certain way – nothing else was needed. An invoice was issued and the other one paid it, and that was it. It was like nothing.'

The new agreement

The new agreement on spare parts for the tails of the Saab 2000 was that Patria Finavicomp Oy would continue to deliver spare parts as long as the aircraft were used in regular traffic. The price agreed for the spare parts was higher than when the aircraft were in production, as in future manufacturing the spare parts would be unit production instead of mass production. In addition, the tools would be taken out of use but could be put back into use for producing spare parts as needed. However, the expected need for spare parts was low. As one of the managers at the Finnish supplier put it: 'These aren't expected to require replacement parts that easily [...] except when they are damaged somewhere in the airfield.'

In the previous extract, the Finnish representative stressed the understanding shared between the business partners. This common ground was partly based on national cultural similarities. Indeed, cross-cultural issues are becoming increasingly important in today's global business, and many projects are global in nature. The international dimension of projects also affects the network pictures and interaction patterns of each party. It therefore becomes critical to consider the special requirements of international Ending Projects. Cultural understanding and sensitivity[11] become especially important when negotiations concern delicate issues in problematic situations, such as termination.

The airline industry, too, is global in nature, which meant that Saab Aircraft AB had customers all over the world (as shown by the lists in Tables 2.1 and 2.2), as well as suppliers in different countries and on different continents. This, in turn, meant that the ending negotiations with the suppliers had to be conducted with partners representing different countries.

The negotiations with the Spanish supplier of wings to Saab 2000 indicate that the parties need to understand each other's way of doing business to be able to come to an agreement (Box 5.7: Terminating a business relationship). As the box illustrates, however, even an understanding of the differences involved will not always help matters to proceed as quickly as the parties would like.

Box 5.7 Terminating a business relationship

The last agreement

The plan was to dissolve the Purchasing Department, which was responsible for renegotiating the contracts with all the roughly 230 suppliers, on 30 June 1999. This proved to be the day when the last renegotiated agreement with a supplier was signed – at 7:00 p.m. The supplier was a Spanish company, CASA Construcciones Aeronauticas, S. A. (referred to below as CASA), which had made the detailed design for the wings of the Saab 2000 and also produced them. CASA was one of the suppliers that would not be able to sell enough spare parts to recover its investment outlay, as a wing does not usually need many spare parts.

Many meetings in eighteen months

The negotiations with CASA took a year and a half. During the negotiation phase, representatives of Saab Aircraft AB and CASA met about ten times in 1998 and six times in 1999. Four persons from CASA and three from Saab Aircraft AB took part in the negotiations. CASA's representatives were from their head office. Saab Aircraft AB was represented by three people: the person with the main responsibility at the Purchasing Department; the purchaser responsible for contacts with CASA; and the controller. These three were authorised to make decisions during the negotiations. The person with the main responsibility at the Purchasing Department expressed it as follows: 'Saab has the great advantage. That one was given authority: "You run this!"'

The negotiators representing Saab Aircraft AB felt that they had more extensive authority to make decisions during the negotiations than the Spanish negotiators appeared to have. The Spanish representatives had to contact their superiors before any decisions were made. One of the Swedish negotiators explained the negotiations in Spain as follows: '... it is typical that one meets on two or three days [...] and then needs to go home and try to see if it is reasonable before confirmation is obtained.' He also felt that negotiating practices in Spain differed from those in other countries: 'They think that it is fun when the situation gets heated, when someone shouts and screams a little, while others, including us, prefer to take it a little more calmly and in a matter-of-fact manner, and proceed step-by-step. But they are not as upset as they sound.' He continued that 'they were very good in separating work and socialising, so we could have dinner together in the evening [...]. And one could see that we were not enemies, we only had different opinions.'

Many details to consider

One reason why these negotiations took so long was that Saab Aircraft AB had placed orders for seventeen wings, which they were now forced to cancel. CASA, in turn, had already ordered material for some of the wings and had started their production. Saab Aircraft AB was prepared to pay for this material, and so CASA and the Saab Aircraft AB representatives together counted all the parts that were ordered as well as what had already been produced. These calculations took a long time because CASA produced the parts in four different factories in Spain. One of the negotiators described the situation as follows: '... a quality engineer [...] was assigned there as long as the deliveries were continuing, and stayed half a year afterwards, too. [...] He visited all the factories there [...]. And then he, our representative, could go to the stores and check that so many parts really did exist.'

Another aspect that called for much discussion and took a long time to reach agreement on was the low production rate. As one of the negotiators stated: 'There was a lot of debate.' The agreement said that if the production rate fell below a certain level, then CASA should be compensated for this. During the last eighteen months, Saab Aircraft AB had purchased fewer wings from CASA than had been agreed. CASA wanted to be compensated accordingly.

Saab Aircraft AB takes over the production of spare parts

Finally, Saab Aircraft AB and CASA agreed that Saab would take over the production of any spare parts that might be needed in future. This was suggested by CASA, as the company did not wish to continue producing spare parts. The parties agreed that the best solution was to transfer the production to a smaller workshop, such as that of Saab Aircraft AB. All the jigs and other tooling were moved from Spain to the Saab premises in Linköping during autumn 1999.

Success in project termination

What counts in the project management is, of course, success. Both researchers and managers are increasingly interested in factors that influence the effectiveness of project management and thus contribute to the success of projects. Several of the issues that influence project effectiveness (that is, the extent to which the project meets its goals) have been discussed. Effectiveness is influenced by, for example, organisational structures, technical competency (tools and methods in project management), leadership ability, and the characteristics of effective project managers.[12] All these seem to be valid also with regard to success in Ending Projects.

A key issue when evaluating project endings is whether the focal companies and key stakeholders are satisfied with the situation afterwards. One concrete indication, of course, is that they can do business together afterwards as well. Still, the project ending may, and often does, lead to several changes affecting the organisations, human resources and even strategies of the company, thereby also affecting the direct and indirect relationships.

Our illustrations give interesting examples, but we want to stress that all Ending Projects are different. In the same way as all business relationships are unique and have different characteristics, there is no single solution to handle their ending. The same applies to projects and their termination. The key is to attend to the critical processes and potential problem areas so that the challenges can be turned into new possibilities.

Key points for managers

- Identify the different types of connections that exist between the stakeholders.
- As stakeholders are connected, they need to be handled simultaneously. The network effects of termination start immediately.
- Stakeholders may be connected to each other indirectly, which means that the connections are not always apparent when observed from the project point of view.
- Indirect connections are among the most difficult issues to handle, as the ending team cannot control them.
- Connections between projects may become a problem during an Ending Project; there is a particular need to analyse the overlap between the network context of the Ending Project and the network contexts of other projects.
- Connections over time affect how the termination process unfolds.
- Drawing network pictures is one way of understanding and managing the connectedness.
- The common norms for behaviour, built up during the initial project in the network context, play an important role when the project is terminated.

Notes

1 See, e.g., Turner, J. R. (1999) *The Handbook of Project-based Management*, 2nd edn, London: McGraw-Hill, p. 361.
2 Halinen, A., Salmi, A. and Havila, V. (1999) 'From Dyadic Change to Changing Business Networks: An Analytical Framework', *Journal of Management Studies*, 36, 779–94; Havila, V. and Salmi, A. (2000) 'Spread of Change in Business Networks: An Empirical Study of Mergers and Acquisitions in the Graphics Industry', *Journal of Strategic Marketing*, 8, 105–19.
3 See, e.g., Anderson, J. C., Håkansson, H. and Johanson, J. (1994) 'Dyadic Business Relationships within a Business Network Context', *Journal of*

Marketing, 58, 1–15; Halinen, Salmi and Havila, op. cit.; Håkansson, H. and Snehota, I. (1989) 'No Business Is an Island: The Network Concept of Business Strategy', *Scandinavian Journal of Management*, 22, 256–70; Håkansson, H. and Snehota, I. (eds) (1995) *Developing Relationships in Business Networks*, London: Routledge.

4 Halinen, Salmi and Havila, op. cit., note that for understanding network dynamics it is crucial to look at these two types of change: radical and incremental. As networks are constantly changing, incremental change takes place on a daily basis, but radical change means that relations are disrupted or established.

5 Lock, D. (2003) *Project Management*, Burlington, USA: Gower.

6 See, e.g., Håkansson and Snehota, 1995, op. cit.

7 Cova, B. and Salle, R. (2005) 'Six Key Points to Merge Project Marketing into Project Management', *International Journal of Project Management*, 23, 357.

8 Ibid.

9 Salmi, A., Havila, V. and Anderson, H. (2001) 'Acquisitions and Network Horizons: A Case Study in the Nordic Graphics Industry', *Nordiske Organisasjonsstudier*, 3, 61–83.

10 Ford, D. *et al.* (2003) *Managing Business Relationships*, 2nd edn, Chichester: John Wiley.

11 Salmi, A. (2007) 'Cultural Sensitivity in International Business Relations: Managerial Skills in Spanning the Finnish–Chinese Cultural Boundaries', *Finanza, Marketing e Produzione*, 25, 7–22.

12 Hyväri, I. (2006) 'Project Management Effectiveness in Project-oriented Business Organizations', *International Journal of Project Management*, 24, 216–25.

6 Conclusions

How to be successful in project ending

This book has investigated project termination: the end phases of projects and the ending of projects. Our discussion has revolved around such issues as ending strategies, ending competence and, finally, management for success in ending.

This final chapter summarises and crystallises our key conclusions. In the first section (What is new in our perspective on projects?), we explain how our approach differs from the dominant project management literature, and describe the additional insight we provide for current and aspiring project managers. In the second section (The uniqueness of the case study in this book), we comment on the real-life case discussed here. So far we have shown how long-term interorganisational co-operation on development and production of aircrafts was terminated and subsequently transformed into an Ending Project. Despite its uniqueness, the case is a good base for learning about projects in general, as it illustrates the many different types of complexities that may be incorporated into Ending Projects.

The sections thereafter concentrate on our central implications for project termination in general; we discuss successively the management of project ending, the ending strategy, ending competence and the organisation for ending. We then focus on the issue of success in project endings and, finally, present the overall conclusions for managers – both general managers as well as (ending) project managers.

What is new in our perspective on projects?

The existing project management literature offers sophisticated tools and techniques for project management, and project managers in general are very skilled in running individual projects and/or project programmes. The literature usually focuses on issues internal to the project. Recent criticisms, however, note that the handbooks and practical guides often fail to recognise that projects have wider contexts.

In this book we concentrate especially on one type of context, namely the network context of a project. We have shown that complicated processes are involved in project termination, largely due to projects not being closed systems. To gain a better understanding of the openness of projects, we have focused on the different stakeholder relationships that may exist in any larger interorganisational project. Our discussion in Chapter 2 shows that each network context of a project is unique and includes project stakeholders as well as other parties that are connected indirectly. All of these may be affected by project termination.

A need to illustrate how project management works in practice has also been expressed. This point has been taken into account here by giving an in-depth report of the developments around a real-life case. The case is revealing, as it shows how much effort the case company invested in involving different partners and in informing and negotiating with external parties. In this case, the management of the project's network context was the key for a successful Ending Project.

Finally, managing a project at the end of its life-cycle is an important phase of project management – and a phase that often gets little attention in project management texts. For project success rates to increase, this phase must also be addressed. Focusing as it does on the often-neglected areas of project management – *the network context, practical guidance for ending projects, as well as the ending phases of projects* – this book is an important addition to conventional project and programme management texts.

The uniqueness of the case study in this book

Projects, project endings and Ending Projects vary. To tackle this variation, we have used one complex case and exposed its complexity by focusing on one facet then another and yet another, and so on. By scrutinising one case – the transformation of long-term production co-operation into an Ending Project and future maintenance of the product – we have managed to give a more vivid account of the connections and dependencies over time and for various parties. The case data have been collected from different sources and through interviews with several individuals working in different organisations.

Even though the case describes a specific situation that occurred in the late 1990s, the results are still visible ten years later: the aircraft continue to fly and the company is doing well in its contemporary business area. (See Figure 6.1: The two planes.)

This makes the case relevant at present, and shows that the strategies adopted and operations implemented in termination were feasible and had long-term positive results. We may therefore conclude that the case illustrates successful management of a project ending.

Figure 6.1 The two planes. Photo courtesy of Saab AB.

In spite of this, we must bear in mind that the case as such may not be a typical example of a project being terminated. The case examined involved complex interorganisational co-operation on product development, production, marketing, and maintenance of aircraft, carried out between different parties. Therefore, rather than presenting the ending phase of a project, the book has shown how a large-scale production programme is terminated and transformed into an Ending Project, and how this Ending Project was executed. The key issue for managers in this case was to ensure the after-sales markets and future business possibilities in new areas.

In its richness, this work contributes to filling the gap in the project management literature and teaching materials dealing with this topic area.

The importance of management

The recent project management literature seems to stress the perspective of leadership, and pays less attention than before to the perspective of task. Our view is on similar lines: leadership and managerial responsibility seem to be especially important in project endings.

We have found that managerial guidebooks pay inadequate attention to managing ending phases or separate Ending Projects. In practice, however, tricky endings are commonplace and, even more importantly, they pose specific managerial challenges. Furthermore, we see these as being related largely to the network context of the Ending Project: project termination means challenges at different levels and in relation to different stakeholders.

To allow a project simply to dissolve is one way of ending it; it may even be the right ending for a project that most of the stakeholders have already 'forgotten' and that they are all ready to let go. In such a case, it is enough to follow the standard advice of project management literature and to end the project in low key. It is then enough to finish the project work, evaluate the project, record the project process, ensure proper archiving and to compile the final report (as noted in Chapter 1). However, this is not the best approach to follow if the project is very large and complicated, if there are several stakeholders interested in the results of the project, and/or if the project needs to be terminated in a way that differs radically from what had initially been planned.

As discussed in Chapter 3, the new situation with its related stress and – often – negative feelings call for sound strategic visions and determination in decision-making from the project owner and/or the general management. These provide a fertile ground for executing the ending.

In project endings, the project management and the general management have different roles. We have stressed the central role of the general management in decision-making pertaining to termination. The general management has the command authority according to a reasonably well-defined managerial hierarchy, while the project management has responsibility without the rank/position. The latter must be able to negotiate win–win results, but in tricky ending situations, empowerment and visible support often need to come from the general management. Therefore, the general management should take the strategic ending decisions (which is not an easy task, as was seen in Chapters 3 and 4), but above all, the general management must give fundamental support to those executing the ending.

The role of the general management is pivotal as support during the Ending Project. Especially if the ending decision is controversial in any way, the general management may be called upon when communicating the message to external stakeholders and internally, and/or when dealing with issues that are negative for some individuals.

Ending strategy

Managerial actions are required when an ongoing project needs to be ended in an unanticipated way. We propose reliance on specific ending strategies and on formulating the managerial situation into a specific Ending Project.

The project termination starts with analysing the network context of the project, which includes the various stakeholders (as discussed in Chapters

2 and 5). Some of the stakeholders are immediate ones that are directly related to the project. There is also a need to consider indirectly connected parties and potential stakeholders. Naturally, any further analysis of the situation needs to be based on screening the knowledge base and vision of the personnel of one's own company.

The three phases of the ending strategy

We propose division of the ending strategy into three phases:

1   Realisation of the need to end a project – this calls for alertness and interpretation of different signals;
2   Planning of the Ending Project – this calls for careful planning based on the special features of ending, such as the project's history, as well as decision-making and commitment at the higher organisational level;
3   Executing the ending project, either by individuals or by teams, in interaction with stakeholders – this calls for special expertise, namely ending competences.

Finally, once the Ending Project has been completed, there is a need for evaluation in order to develop ending competences further and to sharpen the company's alertness to other ending situations that may call for an ending strategy. The company can gradually build up a pool of personnel competent in carrying out endings, as well as know-how and practices for handling the endings efficiently.

Although we have discussed the phases of the ending strategy here, we do not think that managers will get far by first planning and then executing what they have planned. In other words, we do not believe that distinct separations can be made between the phases. In practice, activities need to be taken on several fronts simultaneously. The phase model, however, may make an important contribution by sensitising managers to: the signals indicating the need for project termination; the need for deliberate decision-making; and the importance of support throughout the entire Ending Project.

The right timing is vital

During an Ending Project, different types of processes, or sub-ending projects, take place simultaneously. These processes may follow different timetables and development paths, and to some extent they involve different individuals. This is a challenge for the management, who need to co-ordinate the different processes. Some of the processes are internal to the project; others also involve external parties. Some relate to the initial project, others to its transformation into an Ending Project, and still others focus on expectations for the future.

The timing of information sharing and communication during the various phases of ending is vital. If a large project is terminated in a manner different to that which was originally planned, it is of the utmost importance that the different stakeholders receive accurate information about this directly. This often requires the involvement of the general management. Moreover, the information given must be correct and its sharing must be well co-ordinated. In this way, the company ensures that no incorrect information or rumours start to spread.

The atmosphere changes

In project ending, the goals of many activities are dramatically altered. In consequence, the atmosphere also changes, often from initial inspiration and hype to problems and risks, as discussed in Chapter 4. The management needs to gear thinking so that positive attitudes prevail and ending can have positive outcomes. This is a challenge. To enable continuation, it is critical to maintain people's commitment to the activities that remain to be done immediately or in the future.

Ending Projects are mentally demanding, especially for the 'terminators', i.e. the people responsible for executing the ending. They therefore need exceptional support from their subordinates. The legitimisation for their tasks needs to be made visible as well: the company heroes are usually those who win and start new projects. The ones 'killing' old projects (even when the 'killing' is done softly) are neglected. Yet the 'killers' may play a central role that promotes new deals and future business, as they help to maintain the company's reputation and boost its image.

A pivotal issue for the general management is to make the right decisions with regard to staffing the Ending Project: should the personnel be changed, or to what extent can and should the initiators be involved in terminating the project?

Ending competence

Project endings call for special competence. As defined earlier, project-ending competence means the abilities and skills to close the project so that as little harm as possible is done to the project stakeholders and to indirectly connected parties. As a result, the success of ending depends both on the organisation and on the specific individuals involved.

The company may develop organisational competences, for instance, by formalising the planning and guidance for ending strategies. These might include a time allowance granted by the general manager as well as the preparedness to make decisions and provide support for the ending personnel. At the individual level, some people are by nature better adapted to meeting the challenges of tricky endings and have ending skills which can therefore be developed further, just as any other project management skills.

Today it is easy to find skilful people for the straightforward management of projects. The challenge is to find people equipped to manage the ending of a project in an often highly stressful situation that may involve depressed feelings. Still, in any Ending Project, the termination cannot be entirely outsourced to specialised ending personnel. It is always necessary to know the project features and, for example, the background of interaction in the different relationships that are bound to be affected. Therefore, ending competence means the ability to draw on the knowledge and skills concerning the organisation, the initial project and the external stakeholders, at different levels. All of this know-how should be used to the advantage of ending. To summarise, for ending one needs company-specific, relationship-specific and project-specific knowledge.

Organisation for ending

We noted three key challenges for the management in ending:

1   To retain the key project members and resources.
2   To manage a new type of team (the ending team/organisation).
3   To manage all of the different relations at the same time.

The first two issues are common to any change management situation, and have been widely discussed in the general management literature. The last issue, in turn, can best be handled if the manager understands the connectedness of the relations with the various stakeholders. The manager can, for instance, take advantage of the ideas on network pictures, and can focus on interaction in relationships (as discussed in Chapter 5, in particular).

As we see it, often the best way to handle the challenges is to formulate the task at hand into a new project: the Ending Project. This would have the customary key components of any project: a goal, a budget and a timeline. But as we have shown here, the nature and weight of these components in ending situations differ from those of traditional projects.

It is important to understand the unique features of project endings. There is a difference between the original project and the Ending Project. For instance, project teams often include individuals with a strong conviction in the success of the project. These individuals are therefore not the first to question the project – nor are they necessarily motivated or skilled to execute the termination in practice. Project ending therefore often calls for a separate organisation. The people involved in the initiation and in 'business as usual' are not necessarily the right people to handle the termination. Some authors suggest special 'terminators' or 'exit champions', but in our view these can only partly tackle the challenges.

Whatever the organisation of the ending team, a leader responsible for the Ending Project must be named. Once the strategic decision to end the project has been taken and the general strategy for ending has been defined, the leader needs to plan for termination actively. Good planning, which is also based on the interactive aspects of projects, helps to overcome the challenges typically encountered in ending.

Success in project endings and Ending Projects

Both researchers and managers are becoming increasingly interested in factors that influence project management effectiveness and the success of projects. Several factors have been seen to affect project effectiveness (that is, the extent to which the project attains its goals). These factors include, for instance, organisational structures, tools and methods in project management, leadership and effective project managers. All of these factors seem to play a role in an Ending Project, too.

It is relatively easy to define Ending Project success for the project owner, who takes the decision to opt for ending. However, the more stakeholders and indirectly connected actors there are, the more difficult it becomes to define Ending Project success. The question becomes: Success for whom, and why? The various stakeholders of projects have different agendas. Indeed, this is the area where the real-life case shows its strength. The strategic decision to terminate the production of a product before the break-even point had been reached yielded another type of success, one sign of this being that several of the involved parties seem to be satisfied with both the central company and the end results.

The key reason for satisfaction is the management of the termination. Business actors today are used to changes and are relatively well prepared for them. The project ending may bring about several changes relating to, for example, the organisations, human resources and even strategies of the company. The difference is accomplished by information sharing: We all appreciate being told the reasons for changes and given accurate information, which we, in turn, can use to inform our other counterparts. It is therefore important to take an active role in interacting with the stakeholders rather than to postpone tackling of difficult issues.

An important point when evaluating project endings is whether the focal companies and key stakeholders are satisfied with the situation afterwards. One concrete indication, of course, is that they can later continue working together on other projects. Successful management of ending means future business.

What does it take from the managers?

Throughout the book we have extracted the most important takeaways for managers emerging from our discussion. To summarise the most important issues, we note that in order to achieve success in ending, mostly as related to Ending Project managers, at the operational day-to-day level it takes:

- nerves of steel, to overcome the negative feelings
- teamwork that is geared to the Ending Project and that constitutes a temporary organisation with committed partners with the necessary competences
- continuous work to retain the commitment of the people involved in the Ending Project
- good negotiation skills and active contacts with different parties, and
- the ability to collect and use different types of knowledge, covering the past experiences of the initial situation/project and recent information needed for the new, ending situation.

At the strategic level, meaning the general management, the following considerations are important:

- the courage to make the tough decision to end the project
- attention to different stakeholders early on, and management of relations with them
- the involvement of a sufficiently high managerial level, since the general management needs to give open support to Ending Project managers
- efficient planning for the ending, together with quick and efficient implementation
- information sharing with stakeholders – the information should be given early, it should be relevant and consistent
- the stakeholders are likely to communicate amongst themselves, a probability that should be taken into account
- vision for the future and explicit attempts to learn from earlier ending experiences.

While it is relatively easy to compile checklists for managers, it is an entirely different story to apply all of the good ideas in practice. We have found the real-life case to be exceptionally revealing in showing not only the risks and problems, but also how the management succeeded in tackling them. While we as analysts may extract some lessons to learn for others, we are sure that managers are the most capable of tackling the challenges – if they just decide to do so. We hope this book paves the way for smooth project landings.

Thank you for flying with us!

Bibliography

Alajoutsijärvi, K., Möller, K. and Tähtinen, J. (2000) 'Beautiful Exit: How to Leave Your Business Partner', *European Journal of Marketing*, 34: 1270–90.

Anderson, J. C., Håkansson, H. and Johanson, J. (1994) 'Dyadic Business Relationships within a Business Network Context', *Journal of Marketing*, 58: 1–15.

Cova, B., Mazet, F. and Salle, R. (1996) 'Milieu as a Pertinent Unit of Analysis in Project Marketing', *International Business Review*, 5: 647–64.

Cova, B. and Salle, R. (2005) 'Six Key Points to Merge Project Marketing into Project Management', *International Journal of Project Management*, 23: 354–9.

Dahlin, P. (2007) 'Turbulence in Business Networks: A Longitudinal Study of Mergers, Acquisitions and Bankruptcies Involving Swedish IT Companies', doctoral dissertation, No. 53, Mälardalen University, Sweden.

Davis, D. (2005) 'New Projects: Beware of False Economies', in *Harvard Business Review on Managing Projects*, Boston, Massachusetts: Harvard Business School Publishing Corporation, pp. 19–39. Originally published in *Harvard Business Review*, March–April 1985.

Dwyer, F. R., Schurr, P. H. and Oh, S. (1987) 'Developing Buyer–Seller Relationships', *Journal of Marketing*, 51: 11–27.

Engwall, M. (1995) *Jakten på det effektiva projektet*, Stockholm: Thomson Fakta AB.

Engwall, M. (2003) 'No Project Is an Island: Linking Projects to History and Context', *Research Policy*, 32: 789–808.

Field, M. and Keller, L. (1998) *Project Management*, Oxford: International Thomson Business Press.

Ford, D. (1980) 'The Development of Buyer–Seller Relationships in Industrial Markets', *European Journal of Marketing*, 14: 339–53.

Ford, D. (1998) *Managing Business Relationships*, Chichester, UK: Wiley.

Ford, D., Gadde, L. E., Håkansson, H. and Snehota, I. (2003) *Managing Business Relationships*, 2nd edn, Chichester: John Wiley.

A Guide to the Project Management Body of Knowledge: PMBOK Guide (2004), 3rd edn, Pennsylvania, Project Management Institute.

Giller, C. and Matear, S. (2001) 'The Termination of Inter-firm Relationships', *The Journal of Business & Industrial Marketing*, 16: 94–112.

Håkansson, H. and Snehota, I. (1989) 'No Business Is an Island: The Network Concept of Business Strategy', *Scandinavian Journal of Management*, 22: 256–70.

Håkansson, H. and Snehota, I. (eds) (1995) *Developing Relationships in Business Networks*, London: Routledge.

Halinen, A., Salmi, A. and Havila, V. (1999) 'From Dyadic Change to Changing Business Networks: An Analytical Framework', *Journal of Management Studies*, 36: 779–94.

Halinen, A. and Tähtinen J. (2002) 'A Process Theory of Relationship Ending', *International Journal of Service Industry Management*, 13: 163–80.

Harrison, D. (2004) 'Is a Long-term Business Relationship an Implied Contract? Two Views of Relationship Disengagement', *Journal of Management Studies*, 41: 107–25.

Havila, V. and Salmi, A. (2000) 'Spread of Change in Business Networks: An Empirical Study of Mergers and Acquisitions in the Graphics Industry', *Journal of Strategic Marketing*, 8: 105–19.

Havila, V. and Wilkinson, I. (2002) 'The Principle of the Conservation of Relationship Energy: or Many Kinds of New Beginnings', *Industrial Marketing Management*, 31: 191–203.

Holmlund-Rytkönen, M. and Strandvik, T. (2005) 'Stress in Business Relationships', *Journal of Business & Industrial Marketing*, 20: 12–22.

Hyväri, I. (2006) 'Project Management Effectiveness in Project-oriented Business Organizations', *International Journal of Project Management*, 24: 216–25.

Industrial Marketing and Purchasing Group website: http://www.impgroup.org

Kreiner, K. (1995) 'In Search of Relevance: Project Management in Drifting Environments', *Scandinavian Journal of Management*, 11: 335–46.

Lake, C. (1998) *Mastering Project Management*, Thorogood.

Lock, D. (2003) *Project Management*, Burlington, USA: Gower.

Lundin, R. A. and Söderholm, A. (1995) 'A Theory of the Temporary Organization', *Scandinavian Journal of Management*, 11: 437–55.

Mantel, S. J. Jr, Meredith, J. R., Shafer, S. M. and Sutton, M. M. (2001) *Project Management in Practice*, New York: John Wiley & Sons.

Meredith, J. R. and Mantel, S. J. Jr (2000) *Project Management. A Managerial Approach*, 4th edn, John Wiley & Sons, Inc.

Pressey, A. D. and Mathews, B. P. (2003) 'Jumped, Pushed or Forgotten? Approaches to Dissolution', *Journal of Marketing Management*, 19: 131–55.

Royer, I. (2005) 'Why Bad Projects Are So Hard to Kill', in *Harvard Business Review on Managing Projects*, Boston, Massachusetts: Harvard Business School Publishing Corporation, pp. 85–108. Originally published in *Harvard Business Review*, February 2003.

Saab Aircraft Leasing Market Report, Issue 7, September 1999.

Saab Aircraft. Product information: Saab 2000, http://www.aircraft.saab.se/proinf/s2000, 1999-03-25.

Sahlin-Andersson, K. and Söderholm, A. (eds) (2002) *Beyond Project Management: New Perspectives on the Temporary–Permanent Dilemma*, Liber, Abstrakt and Copenhagen Business School.

Salmi, A. (2007) 'Cultural Sensitivity in International Business Relations: Managerial Skills in Spanning the Finnish–Chinese Cultural Boundaries', *Finanza, Marketing e Produzione*, 25: 7–22.

Salmi, A., Havila, V. and Anderson, H. (2001) 'Acquisitions and Network Horizons: A Case Study in the Nordic Graphics Industry', *Nordiske Organisasjonsstudier*, 3: 61–83.

Söderlund, J. (2005) *Projektledning & projektkompetens. Perspektiv på konkurrenskraft*, Malmö: Liber AB.

Spirer, H. F. and Hamburger, D. H. (1988) 'Phasing Out the Project', in Cleland, D.

I. and King, W. R. (eds) *Project Management Handbook*, 2nd edn, New York: Van Nostrand Reinhold, pp. 231–50.

Staw, B. M. and Ross, J. (2005) 'Knowing When to Pull the Plug', in *Harvard Business Review on Managing Projects*, Massachusetts: Harvard Business School Publishing Corporation, pp. 65–84. Originally published in *Harvard Business Review*, March–April 1987.

Tähtinen, J. (2001) 'The Dissolution Process of a Business Relationship: A Case Study from Tailored Software Business', doctoral dissertation, Acta Universitatis Ouluensis G. Oeconomica 10, Oulu.

Tähtinen, J. and Halinen, A. (2002) 'Research on Ending Exchange Relationships: A Categorization, Assessment and Outlook', *Marketing Theory*, 2: 165–88.

Turner, J. R. (1999) *The Handbook of Project-based Management*, 2nd edn, London: McGraw-Hill.

Williams, T., Ackermann, F., Eden, C. and Howick, S. (2005) 'Learning from Project Failure', in Love, P., Fong, P. S. W. and Irani, Z. (eds) *Management of Knowledge in Project Environments*, Oxford: Elsevier, pp. 219–36.

Index

For Product Safety Concerns and Information please contact our EU
representative GPSR@taylorandfrancis.com
Taylor & Francis Verlag GmbH, Kaufingerstraße 24, 80331 München, Germany